When
Congress Debates

When Congress Debates

A Bakhtinian Paradigm

Theodore F. Sheckels

Praeger Series in Political Communication

Westport, Connecticut
London

Library of Congress Cataloging-in-Publication Data

Sheckels, Theodore F.
    When Congress debates : a Bakhtinian paradigm / Theodore F. Sheckels.
        p.   cm.—(Praeger series in political communication, ISSN 1062–5623)
    Includes bibliographical references and index.
    ISBN 0–275–96667–4 (alk. paper)
        1. Communication in politics—United States.   2. Political oratory—United States.   3.
    Debates and debating—United States.   4. United States. Congress.   5. Bakhtin, M. M.
    (Mikhail Mikhaælovich), 1895–1975.   I. Title.   II. Series.
    JA85.2.U6S54   2000
    328.73′02—dc21   00–036708

British Library Cataloguing in Publication Data is available.

Library of Congress Catalog Card Number: 00–036708
ISBN: 0–275–96667–4
ISSN: 1062–5623

First published in 2000

Praeger Publishers, 88 Post Road West, Westport, CT 06881
An imprint of Greenwood Publishing Group, Inc.
www.praeger.com

Printed in the United States of America

The paper used in this book complies with the
Permanent Paper Standard issued by the National
Information Standards Organization (Z39.48–1984).

10 9 8 7 6 5 4 3 2 1

Copyright Acknowledgments

Contents

Series Foreword

Those of us from the discipline of communication studies have long believed that communication is prior to all other fields of inquiry. In several other forums I have argued that the essence of politics is "talk" or human interaction.[1] Such interaction may be formal or informal, verbal or nonverbal, public or private, but it is always persuasive, forcing us consciously or subconsciously to interpret, to evaluate, and to act. Communication is the vehicle for human action.

From this perspective, it is not surprising that Aristotle recognized the natural kinship of politics and communication in his writings *Politics* and *Rhetoric*. In the former, he established that humans are "political beings, [who] alone of the animals [are] furnished with the faculty of language."[2] In the latter, he began his systematic analysis of discourse by proclaiming that "rhetorical study, in its strict sense, is concerned with the modes of persuasion."[3] Thus, it was recognized over twenty-three hundred years ago that politics and communication go hand in hand because they are essential parts of human nature.

In 1981, Dan Nimmo and Keith Sanders proclaimed that political communication was an emerging field.[4] Although its origin, as noted, dates back centuries, a "self-consciously cross-disciplinary" focus began in the late 1950s. Thousands of books and articles later, colleges and universities offer a variety of graduate and undergraduate coursework in the area in such diverse departments as communication, mass communication, journalism, political science, and sociology.[5] In Nimmo and Sanders' early assessment, the "key areas of inquiry" included rhetorical analysis, propaganda analy-

sis, attitude change studies, voting studies, government and the news media, functional and systems analyses, technological changes, media
technologies, campaign techniques, and research techniques.[6] In a survey
of the state of the field in 1983, the same authors and Lynda Kaid found additional, more specific areas of concerns such as the presidency, political
polls, public opinion, debates, and advertising.[7] Since the first study, they
have also noted a shift away from the rather behavioral approach.

A decade later, Dan Nimmo and David Swanson argued that "political
communication has developed some identity as a more or less distinct domain of scholarly work."[8] The scope and concerns of the area have further
expanded to include critical theories and cultural studies. Although there is
no precise definition, method, or disciplinary home of the area of inquiry, its
primary domain comprises the role, processes, and effect of communication within the context of politics broadly defined.

In 1985, the editors of *Political Communication Yearbook: 1984* noted
that "more things are happening in the study, teaching, and practice of political communication than can be captured within the space limitations of the
relatively few publications available."[9] In addition, they argued that the
backgrounds of "those involved in the field [are] so varied and pluralist in
outlook and approach, . . . it [is] a mistake to adhere slavishly to any set format in shaping the content."[10] More recently, Swanson and Nimmo have
called for "ways of overcoming the unhappy consequences of fragmenta-
tion within a framework that respects, encourages, and benefits from diverse scholarly commitments, agendas, and approaches."[11]

In agreement with these assessments of the area and with gentle encourage-
ment, in 1988 Praeger established the series entitled "Praeger Series in Political
Communication." The series is open to all qualitative and quantitive methodol-
ogies as well as contemporary and historical studies. The key to characterizing
the studies in the series is the focus on communication variables or activities
within a political context or dimension. As of this writing, over seventy vol-
umes have been published and numerous impressive works are forthcoming.
Scholars from the disciplines of communication, history, journalism, political
science, and sociology have participated in the series.

I am, without shame or modesty, a fan of the series. The joy of serving as
its editor is in participating in the dialogue of the field of political communication and in reading the contributors' works. I invite you to join me.

Robert E. Denton, Jr.

NOTES

    1. See Robert E. Denton, Jr., *The Symbolic Dimensions of the American
Presidency* (Prospect Heights, IL: Waveland Press, 1982); Robert E. Denton, Jr.,

and Gary Woodward, *Political Communication in America* (New York: Praeger, 1985; 2d ed., 1990); Robert E. Denton, Jr., and Dan Hahn, *Presidential Communication* (New York: Praeger, 1986); and Robert E. Denton, Jr., *The Primetime Presidency of Ronald Reagan* (New York: Praeger, 1988).

2. Aristotle, *The Politics of Aristotle*, trans. Ernest Barker (New York: Oxford University Press, 1970), p. 5

3. Aristotle, *Rhetoric*, trans. W. Rhys Roberts (New York: The Modern Library, 1954), p. 22.

4. Dan Nimmo and Keith Sanders, "Introduction: The Emergence of Political Communication as a Field," in H*andbook of Political Communication*, eds. Dan Nimmo and Keith Sanders (Beverly Hills, CA: Sage, 1981), pp. 11–36.

5. Ibid., p. 15.

6. Ibid., pp. 17–27.

7. Keith Sanders, Lynda Kaid, and Dan Nimmo, eds., *Political Communication Yearbook: 1984* (Carbondale, IL: Southern Illinois University, 1985), pp. 283–308.

8. Dan Nimmo and David Swanson, "The Field of Political Communication: Beyond the Voter Persuasion Paradigm," in *New Directions in Political Communication*, eds. David Swanson and Dan Nimmo (Beverly Hills, CA: Sage, 1990), p. 8.

9. Sanders, Kaid, and Nimmo, *Political Communication Yearbook: 1984*, p. xiv

10. Ibid.

11. Nimmo and Swanson, "The Field of Political Communication," p. 11.

Preface

Political communication scholars understandably devote much time to studying the conduct of elections, for they are a fascinating topic. And, in many cases, it is a fascination with the high-profile campaigns that has led many scholars to choose to do their work in political communication. However, there are other areas of political communication that now demand attention. One of these is the debating that occurs in legislatures—the U.S. Senate and the U.S. House of Representatives or those in the various states. At least part of this particular communication arena's demand on scholarly attention is tied to the fact (yes, the fact) that it has been largely ignored by the communication discipline.

There are many reasons why debates in the nation's legislative bodies have been overlooked. One, I think, is that the dominance of a bipolar paradigm has obscured from view the rhetorical richness of these debates. Humans necessarily find convenient ways to process messy material in order to make sense of it. And pro vs. con—Democrat vs. Republican—has been over the years a convenient way to transform hours, if not days, of talking into something manageable.

Once reduced to something manageable, however, these debates no longer seem especially interesting. The work of Russian literary theorist Mikhail Bakhtin offers the political communication scholar a new way to see these debates, a way that reveals their richness. Using a Bakhtinian paradigm, a scholar would put bipolarity in its proper place (and it does have a place). Rather than giving primacy to an oppositional construct, a scholar would explore all of the voices that comprise the debate's polyphony, including both the many speakers themselves and the voices they sound by citing, quoting, using the famous words of, telling constituents' stories, and inventing the words someone or some group might utter. Using a Bakhtinian paradigm, a scholar would also look for the use of double-voiced discourse and the eruption of carnivalesque energy, especially when these serve to subvert the established order. A scholar would also refuse to see these debates as finalizable and would look beyond the artificial temporal boundaries on both ends.

When Congress Debates fleshes out how a scholar or critic would proceed if alert to the multi-voiced nature of all utterances and if aware of how all words and phrases have been previously voiced in specific contexts and, therefore, carry entailments that may function in the polyphony of the Congressional chambers. Chapter One reviews the existing literature on debates in the House and the Senate. After exploring why these studies are so limited, the chapter focuses on a handful of analyses that suggest what a fuller examination of Congressional debating might reveal. Chapter Two extracts from the work of Mikhail Bakhtin a critical methodology designed to serve as a heuristic that will prompt just such a fuller examination. Chapter Two, I should note, is not intended to be an essay about theory. Rather, it explores Bakhtin just enough so that the reader understands how the recommended paradigm is rooted in what the Russian theorist said. Not all concepts in Bakhtin's oeuvre are covered; the chapter does not substitute for a close reading of Bakhtin's texts or the several good commentaries on those texts.

Chapters Three through Seven offer five case studies of debates in the U.S. Senate. These case studies are not arranged chronologically. Rather, they are arranged by the duration of the debate—shortest to longest. One of the difficulties facing a political communication scholar who wishes to study Congressional debating is that many of the debates are quite unwieldy. No matter what paradigm she or he may follow, the briefer the debate, the easier will be the application. I therefore begin with the easier cases—Illinois Senator Carol Moseley-Braun's 1993 attempt to deny Senate sanction to the Daughters of the Confederacy's use of the Confederate flag in Chapter Three and the seven female Senators' 1994 attempt to deny Frank B. Kelso II a retirement rank of four-star admiral in Chapter Four. The latter question took slightly longer than six hours on the Senate floor.

Chapter Five examines a debate that developed over several days in 1995. Although many spoke, the core of the debate is a duel between California Senator Barbara Boxer and New Hampshire Senator Bob Smith over what pro-life forces termed "partial-birth abortion."

Chapters Six and Seven look at still longer debates. These two chapters return us to the 1960s. Chapter Six examines an early 1960 debate over the poll tax still in place in a handful of states. Chapter Seven examines a late 1969 debate over a controversial Supreme Court nomination made by President Richard Nixon, the nomination of Clement F. Haynsworth, Jr., of South Carolina.

These five debates were selected because they are interesting. They were also selected because I wanted to, at least partially, build on existing scholarship, good scholarship that is not as good as it could be because all of the questions that emerge from a Bakhtinian paradigm are not being addressed. Thus, foregrounding my discussion of Carol Moseley-Braun's carnivalesque subversion of Senate norms is John Butler's 1995 essay on the debate in *Argumentation and Advocacy*; foregrounding my discussion of the female use of intertexts and double-voiced discourse in the Senate women's rejection of high honors for Kelso is my own 1997 essay in the *Southern Communication Journal*. Very much in view in my Chapter Six analysis of the debate over the poll tax is Ernest Bormann's 1962 *Southern Speech Journal* essay on another 1960 debate over a civil rights matter that led to a rhetorically interesting filibuster. I try to discuss debating strategy, much as Bormann does, but I also explore the filibuster as carnivalesque— something Bakhtin alerts us to. And very much in view in my Chapter Seven analysis of the debate over Haynsworth's nomination is Richard Vatz and Theodore Windt's 1974 *Quarterly Journal of Speech* essay on both the Haynsworth and the later Carswell debates. I try to show how their "need" to construct a bipolar reading resulted in a mis-reading. I also try to expand upon their awareness of the double-voicing occurring in these related debates. Not being aware of Bakhtin's concept of double-voiced discourse, I argue, limited what they might say about arguments that were not ever voiced but, nonetheless, seemed very present in the debates.

Chapters Five and Eight are the exception: they do not play off of existing scholarship. They deal with the two most recent debates. The debate over "partial-birth abortion" struck me as one that was ripe for Bakhtinian analysis because of the way Senator Boxer and others attempted to bring the voices and the faces of women into the debate. Her use of photographs to counter Senator Smith's anatomical charts struck me as a "classic" example of parodic double-voiced discourse the moment I saw it presented on the network news in 1995. The debate over the impeachment of President Clinton struck me as worth analyzing because of the ways the different rhetors were using inter-voices. In addition, I wanted to examine at least one debate from the House of Representatives so I could demonstrate that the Bakhtinian paradigm is useful no matter which side of "The Hill" you're on.

The "test" of a critical perspective is not, I would suggest, the extent to which it illuminates the dark corners of discourse. Quite frankly, when I read such illuminations, I wonder whether what was found in those dark corners really functioned—in any meaningful way—in the discourse. Rather, the "test" should be the extent to which a perspective or paradigm offers an accurate, full description and reveals the rhetorical richness of whatever is being analyzed. I believe the case studies presented in *When Congress Debates* demonstrate that a Bakhtinian approach does indeed offer such an analysis. Some of the highlights that I glanced at above in reviewing the book's contents should suggest as much. With the help of Bakhtin's ideas, we see Carol Moseley-Braun orchestrating carnivalesque subversion, the women of the Senate using very different inter-voices than the men, Barbara Boxer using visual double-voiced discourse to parody Bob Smith's faceless diagrams, Southern Senators' displaying a learned carnivalesque irreverence as they almost-filibuster against a ban on the poll tax, Southern Senators' responding to the unvoiced entailments of the arguments being offered against Haynsworth, and members of the House fighting over the inter-voices of Abe Lincoln, Jesus Christ, and Bob Dole.

The ideas presented in these analyses have developed over years. An earlier version of some of what is now Chapter Four was presented at the 1995 Speech Communication Association convention in San Antonio and is published in the *Southern Communication Journal*. Its editor, Craig A. Smith, and its anonymous readers helped me refine my ideas. Earlier versions of the book as a whole were presented at the 1998 Southern States Speech Communication Association meeting in San Antonio and the 1998 National Communication Association convention in New York City. Some of the ideas in Chapters Three, Four, and Five were presented as part of a paper on empowering discourse at the 1999 Eastern Communication Association meeting in Charleston, West Virginia. Readers for *Rhetoric and Public Affairs* and the *Quarterly Journal of Speech* helped me refine my ideas and my approach. They also convinced me that only a book-length presentation could do my subject justice. Three colleagues have helped improve the manuscript of this book through their judicious comments. I thank Carole Blair of the University of California, Davis; Janette Kenner Muir of George Mason University; and Judith S. Trent of the University of Cincinnati for their help. I also thank Robert E. Denton, Jr., general editor of the Praeger Series in Political Communication, for his support of this project, and James T. Sabin, Leanne Small, and Linda Ellis-Stiewing at the Greenwood Publishing Group for their work speeding this book toward publication. I would like to acknowledge the financial support I received from the Walter Williams Craigie Endowment of Randolph-Macon College during two summers—to work on the *Southern Communication Journal* article of which Chapter Four is a significant revision and, then, to draft the manuscript of this book.

Chapter One

Congressional Debating:
A Neglected Subject

Congressional debating is of consequence. The matters that are before the Senate and the House of Representatives touch on peace and war, prosperity and poverty, security and anxiety. Although it is indeed true that much decision-making occurs in venues other than the respective floors, nonetheless, the floor debates do present, in somewhat crystallized forms, positions on these matters for both fellow legislators and the general public to consider. C-SPAN and C-SPAN 2 have made these positions more readily available to both of these audiences. Furthermore, these debates have implications beyond the matters immediately at hand, setting the agenda for future policy-making as well as for future elections.

Unfortunately, if one studies these floor debates, either in person sitting in the gallery or through the pages of the *Congressional Record*, much of what one discovers interferes with analysis as well as appreciation. There is long-windedness and repetition; there are times when the hall is virtually empty and times when the legislators present are engaged in distracting conversations. But what truly interferes is the observer's assumptions: that debates have clearly defined affirmative and negative sides and that debates proceed, snappily, through a predesignated format to a win or lose conclusion. In other words, what interferes is the unvoiced assumption that Congressional debates are like academic debates. And, when they prove not to be, observers often reject them, denigrating them as less than debates or something other than debates. Either that or observers force what they see or read to conform to the definition of the debate genre they bring to the task. These observers do not think of revising their definition of "debates" to fit what they see or read. Put another way, they do not think that the paradigm they bring to the task may be in need of substantial revision if they are to appreciate the rhetorical richness that Congressional debating does exhibit.

That such a new paradigm is necessary is suggested by the literature since the 1940s on Congressional debating. This chapter will review that literature. Although an occasional article has attempted to discuss a particular debate as departing from the norm and being significant, most conclude that the debating is both tedious and inconsequential. I wish to suggest that the prevailing paradigm has played a telling role in limiting the analysis thus far and thereby has produced negative assessments.

EARLY ASSESSMENTS

In 1941, John R. Fitzpatrick presented what still remains the consensus concerning debating in Congress in an essay entitled—appropriately enough—"Congressional Debating" in the *Quarterly Journal of Speech*. He noted that the speeches are not "good reads" and that they do not significantly affect voting (252). He refused to even label what he saw as "debating"; rather, it was just "talking" (251). Seven years later, writing for the same journal, Jerry Voorhis offered a somewhat different assessment. He agreed with Fitzpatrick that the speeches were not compelling, but he argued that the speeches were so because they lacked "style." They were not "oratory." The rhetorical situation in the Senate or House, Voorhis argued, required chains of arguments with supporting facts, not eloquence (462–63). One can infer from his essay that he believed public policy decision-making was being practiced during floor debates and that public policy decision-making and effective speech-making were for some unexplained reason opposed. So, whereas Fitzpatrick and Voorhis seemed to disagree about the value of what they saw occurring on Capitol Hill, neither saw it as being a communication activity worthy of study. It wasn't debate; it wasn't oratory.

Scholarship in the communication field in the 1940s did not exhibit the rigor it does today; therefore, it should not be entirely surprising that neither Fitzpatrick nor Voorhis offered much in the way of evidence for their conclusions. In the next two decades, there were some attempts to gather the necessary evidence.

Earl R. Cain wrote two similar essays in the mid-1950s on the topic. The first, "A Method for Rhetorical Analysis of Congressional Debate," appeared in *Western Speech* in 1954; the second, "Is Senate Debate Significant," appeared on the opposite coast in *Today's Speech* in 1955. Both essays reviewed the literature on the question up to that time and noted how Congressional debating is usually disparaged. Then, the essays play off of two published case studies to suggest that debating is not without some impact. The case studies, discussed more fully later in this chapter, are Ralph Micken's 1951 analysis of the debate over the United States' membership in the League of Nations in the *Quarterly Journal of Speech* and Giraud Chester's 1945 analysis of the pre-World War II debates over neutrality in the same journal. The former debate, Cain noted, played an important albeit vague role "in expressing and in determining national policy" ("A Method": 92). By this phrase, Cain seemed to have a dual function in mind: educating the public and assuring that policy options were "studied from all sides" ("Is Senate Debate": 10–12). The latter debate actually featured floor speeches that influenced votes!

At the same time Cain offered these cases as evidence that Congressional debate had value, however, he demurred. With regards to the first case, he said, "It must be admitted that a direct causal relationship between Senate debate and any shift or strengthening of public opinion is most difficult to discover" ("Is Senate Debate": 11); on the latter, he noted that, "By the very nature of our system of representative government, with its political parties, pressure groups, loyalties, and secret committee decisions, it is a fairly impossible task to isolate a speech on the Senate floor and to claim that this speech was a significant factor in the final voting" ("Is Senate Debate": 12). So, Cain, in a sense, took away what he gave by demurring so.

Henry Z. Scheele, writing in the February 1966 *Today's Speech*, offered what some might term firmer conclusions because they were based, not in case studies, but on empirical research—specifically, questionnaires he sent to selected House members in 1961 and in 1964. In general, the responding legislators did not boost the image of Congressional debating. Many cited how "positions on legislation are often formulated during the committee stage of legislative development" and how "many votes are arranged along party lines" (20). Nonetheless, some respondents could point to some specific floor speeches (for example, Charles Halleck on agricultural policy, Hale Boggs on trade, and Wilbur Mills on tax policy) or some specific speakers (for example, Sam Rayburn) who could make a difference (20). Scheele's conclusion is that the speeches that comprise floor debates have "a moderate effect on legislation" (20).

Similar in methodology are a series of studies in 1959, 1967, and 1979 by D. Dudley Cahn and others. The last such study, reported in *Communication Quarterly*, noted that speeches in committees and interpersonal communication were equally influential in the opinion of surveyed members of the Senate. These Senators felt in 1979, as in 1959 and 1967, that floor speeches exerted very little influence on voting. Nonetheless, they felt that going on the record through floor speeches was important (50–51). The questionnaire did not allow these respondents to specify why.

In 1995, a decade and a half after the last reported survey, some of the same questions of efficacy are raised in a special issue of *Argumentation and Advocacy*, edited by Thomas Kane. Between 1979 and 1995, the communication discipline largely ignored Congressional debating. The literature in political science, however, did address the subject. Several studies, notably those by Michael J. Robinson and Kevin R. Appel in the *Political Science Quarterly*; Arthur H. Miller, Edie N. Goldenberg, and Lutz Erbring in the *American Political Science Review*; and Charles Tidmarch and John C. Pitney, Jr., in *Polity*, reported how media coverage of Congressional debates had declined and how the limited coverage was usually negative. Journalism scholar Richard Davis' essay in *Television Quarterly* concurred. Davis in *The Press and American Politics* (1992) attempted to explain the paucity and the negativity. The paucity, Davis argues, was because the press felt that "real" policy-making was engaged in by leaders off the floor and by leaders and others in committee work. Therefore, coverage shifted to interviews with leaders and snippets from hearings. Sound bites from floor debates usually added the "color" of emotional bombast and very little more.

BARRIERS TO ANALYSIS

All of the literature reviewed thus far has focused on the question of whether Congressional debating was worth attending to. But the literature in communication points to another issue: Even if we grant that Senate and House debates ought to be studied because of their role in public policy-making, these debates are difficult to analyze, for, as Janice Schuetz and Thomas Kane have suggested in separate articles in *Argumentation and Advocacy*, Congressional debates are too often characterized by ritualistic reference and deference and lengthy discussions of procedural matters. But whereas Kane treated these as annoying barriers to analysis in his brief editor's introduction to the Fall 1995 special issue of *Argumentation and Advocacy*, Schuetz, in her attempt to define Congressional debate as a distinct argument field, saw them as a reflection of one of the debates' three audiences. Members of Congress, as Schuetz saw the matter, spoke to their colleagues, to constituents, and to the media. To the extent rhetors offered the elements of a good story (for example, partisan clash, human interest), they were addressing the media; to the extent rhetors offered salient appeals, they were addressing constituents, and, when rhetors ritualistically referred or deferred or negotiated rules of procedure, they were addressing their peers in the Congress. Understanding that these "overlays" (to use Schuetz's term) reflect the needs of different audiences turns the tedious into the rhetorically understandable.

Scholars, such as Peter Kane writing in 1971 in the *Quarterly Journal of Speech*, have also noted the repetition and lack of clash. These elements, which would damn an academic debate to the rubbish heap, may be easily explained if one abandons the academic debate model and grasps certain givens about floor debates in Congress: specifically, that initial speeches on a topic are usually scripted position papers and, therefore, not intended to be responsive to other speeches and that legislators wander in and out of the chamber and may likely not have been present to hear much of the debate that preceded their own scripted addresses. One must work one's way past these "set" pieces to get to the clash. This process is exacerbated by how the debates, as several have noted, are often extended over periods of days or weeks (Chester; Cain, "Is Senate Debate"; Peter Kane; Schuetz). Rare are debates, such as the first two considered in this book, that are neatly confined to a certain period within a single day. Much more common are diffuse debates such as those examined in Chapters Five, Six, and Seven. An understanding of Congressional debate as a genre or argument field helps the scholar to tolerate the tedium. Nothing but patience is available, however, to the scholar who traces a debate that proceeds across several days or longer.

I want to suggest that still another barrier to analysis is the way in which critics bring assumptions true of academic debate to their analysis of Congressional debates. Critics assume that, once you get to the core of the debate, you will find a clash that can be accurately rendered in bipolar terms. This assumption functions much like a paradigm in almost all studies of Congressional debates. In his address to the 1988 Republican national convention, Ronald Reagan quoted John Adams as saying "Facts are stubborn things." Well, paradigms are also stubborn things. And this rather simple bipolar paradigm has governed almost all discussion of political communication in the legislative arena. This paradigm is rooted in how legislative debates are structured, reinforced by how they are reported, and exhibited time and time again in analyses. And to the extent these studies establish a critical norm, they further reinforce the paradigm.

Debates on the floor of a legislative assembly are framed by rules. Thus, for any matter under discussion, there are two sides, and the procedures usually attempt to balance the discourse for the one side against the discourse for the other. For example, time is often equally allocated, and each side has someone managing its time. News media reports on debates reinforce this bipolarity by listing votes as aye or nay. And, although the two bipolarities do not match up, the discourse is often framed—by the media—in Democratic vs. Republican terms. As Richard Davis noted in *The Press and American Politics*, the media tend to present Congressional debates in political terms and gravitate to the leaders of the two parties for commentary from the presumed two sides. Furthermore, we all know that there are two sides of the aisle—majority vs. minority: the physical layout of the chamber, then, reinforces bipolarity. The discussions are, of course, called debates, and debates are two-sided things (as well as stubborn things). Rules and procedures suggest bipolarity; reporting conventions suggest and reinforce bipolarity. Not surprisingly, published studies seem imprisoned by it.

In 1945, Chester examined the Senate debate on the Selective Training and Service Bill of 1940. He talked in terms of "Both sides in the debate" (408); he even spoke of "The affirmative strategy" and "The strategy of the negative" (408). In fact, at times, Chester sounded as if he were introducing an academic debate—for example, when noting the leaders of the affirmative and negative sides.

In 1951 and 1952, Micken examined the 1919–20 debate over the League of Nations. Although very aware of the extra-Senate campaigning going on and seeing this communication as part of the debate, he framed the debate in terms of pro- and anti-League sides. Micken's language was very bipolar: "both sides"; "on the pro-League side"; "on the anti-League side"; "considerable stress was placed by affirmative forces." His language was also, like Chester's, suggestive of an academic debate. For example, when explaining the absence of the equivalent of a first affirmative constructive speech on the part of the pro-League side, Chester says, "It is almost as if the pro-League Senators felt that, a prima facie case having been made by the President and Mr. Taft, theirs was simply the task of rebuttal. They entered into the argument only to reinforce the case after it has been attacked" (50–51).

Let me emphasize that the problem with the bipolar paradigm is that it superimposes a structure on the debate. That structure privileges elements in the debate that readily fit it; however, the structure marginalizes or ignores elements that do not. In the case of the League of Nations debate, persuasive activities going on beyond the confines of the Senate were very important. Micken mentioned them, but they became quite marginal as his analysis proceeded. That analysis focused on the two sides in the debate. There were also, as his 1952 essay in *Western Speech* suggests, noteworthy individual voices during the floor debate. They were lost in the bipolar analysis of the *Quarterly Journal of Speech* article; they were almost lost in the *Western Speech* essay, which was not an analysis of the debate but, rather, a series of portraits of noteworthy Western participants in it. He offered portraits but offered these within a bipolar con-pro framework, a framework that strikes a reader as awkward since Micken seemed to be straining to find pro Senators to balance William E. Borah of Idaho and Hiram Johnson of California. Micken, of course, did not need to use a con-pro structure at all. Nonpartisanship probably blended with the nagging bipolar paradigm to produce the essay's con-pro structure.

In 1955, Cain ("A Method") outlined a method for analyzing Congressional debates. He explicitly deflected critical attention away from the many voices involved by arguing that "the analysis of individual speeches is unlikely to be productive of useful results" (93). Instead, the critic should pay attention to "the arguments, evidence, and special appeals on each side of the question" and thereby arrive at an understanding of "the argumentative process used by both sides" (94). Note how "each" became "both." "The most significant section of the [critical] work," Cain argued, "should be a summary of the argument, evidence, and appeals in the opposing positions" (95). Although some of Cain's language admitted the theoretical possibility of multiple voices, much of that language betrayed his unvoiced assumption that debates consisted, by definition, of two opposing sides.

POST-1960 ANALYSES

The analyses after 1960 were more sophisticated. Braden, writing in 1960 on the League of Nations debate, saw four groups, not two—one in favor; three against. But, by the conclusion of his article, he was talking in the bipolar terms of "pro-League Senators" (278) and "the opponents of the League" (279). In doing so, Braden neglected the public education campaign pro-League political leaders were conducting as the Senate debate proceeded. Braden also understated President Wilson's role in the larger debate, although he did acknowledge that the president had delivered the equivalent of the first affirmative constructive speech before the floor debate commenced.

Bormann, writing in 1962, on an anti-civil rights filibuster in early 1960, saw a pro-civil rights bloc comprised of three groups pitted against an anti-civil rights bloc of Southern Senators:

> The Senate civil rights bloc was divided into three groups: (1) the Republican regulars, headed by minority leader Dirksen, fighting for the Administration's omnibus civil rights bill, (2) the Democratic moderates from the border and western states under the leadership of Lyndon Johnson, and (3) a coalition of Republicans and Democrats,

representing the urban-industrial states of the North and West, who wanted a broader bill than the Administration's omnibus bill.

Opposed to this coalition of civil rights advocates were eighteen senators from the old Confederacy, representing Florida, Georgia, South Carolina, North Carolina, Virginia, Alabama, Mississippi, Louisiana, and Arkansas. (184)

He avoided collapsing the three pro-civil rights groups, probably because strategic divisions among them led to their defeat. In fact, it was several moves by the most liberal faction, including its unsuccessful effort to invoke cloture, that precipitated the collapse:

On March 8, the liberal revolt took place. They presented a cloture petition with thirty-one names, almost twice the requisite number. Both Johnson and Dirksen fought the cloture saying that it was premature. . . .

On March 11, the House began to work on its civil rights bill and the next day the liberal bloc's strategy exploded in their faces as the Senate voted against cloture 53 to 42. The vote was a psychological disaster from which the liberals never recovered. . . . After the vote on cloture and the defeat of part three which followed in the same day, the liberal position became untenable. (190–91)

The voices on the pro-civil rights side retained some of their distinctiveness in Bormann's account, despite its overarching bipolarity. However, he stressed the Southern bloc's successful strategies so much that the multi-voicedness of the pro-civil rights group became somewhat lost, as did the stylistically different efforts of Senators Dirksen of Illinois and Johnson of Texas to sustain the coalition and prevent parliamentary maneuvering led by Senator Russell of Georgia. What does not become obscured are the different voices within that Southern bloc.

The stereotypical filibuster has a Senator or a group of Senators reading the Washington, DC telephone directory for hour after hour. But, as Bormann notes, "This was not Huey Long reading from the woman's underwear section of a mail order catalogue" (187). Such a filibuster might well have provoked a successful cloture vote. So the Southern bloc actually presented well-reasoned albeit drawn out argumentation. As Bormann saw the debate, the Southern bloc had four distinct classes of argument, and each class had its spokesman. Thus, offering the legal argument was Sam Ervin of North Carolina, offering the constitutional argument was Harry Byrd of

Virginia, offering the practical argument was Spressard Holland of Florida, and offering the moral argument was James Eastland of Mississippi. Since Bormann's point was that the Southerners orchestrated this filibuster from a strategic as well as a rhetorical perspective, he kept the four lines of arguments and the four separate speakers relatively distinct. They do not fold into the con side of a bipolar analysis, although the success the essay touts is clearly attributed to the bloc of opposed Senators presented as a side in the debate, not as eighteen distinct voices. Bormann's analysis then walks the tightrope between bipolarity and the plurality of voices—and does so successfully.

Nineteen sixty was indeed a "big" year for civil rights debates in the Congress. Rather than waiting for the very uncertain results of the 1960 election, progressive legislators were seizing opportunities to enact large or small civil rights laws. Bormann revealed how rich a March debate was. He did so by discussing the strategies used by both sides; however, he also did so by not neglecting the different voices that comprised those supposed sides. The individual rhetors are rarely obscured in his analysis. Certainly more could be said about that filibuster. For example, the voices the several Senators chose to invoke as they spoke could be profitably examined. However, rather than reconsider the debate Bormann analyzed reasonably well, a later chapter in this book will examine, using a Bakhtinian paradigm, an earlier 1960 civil rights debate. Some of what that chapter will show—the kinds of voices the Southern Senators introduced into the debate, their use of double-voice discourse, and their use of the carnivalesque—is equally true of the March filibuster. In fact, the January–February debate over the poll tax might be considered a trial run for the March debate Bormann studied.

Walter R. Fisher, writing in 1966, on Senator John J. Crittenden's proposed compromise in 1860–61, was not as successful as Bormann had been in avoiding the trap of bipolarity. When analyzing this compromise, one that might have averted the Civil War, Fisher saw two "rival factions" (367). Yes, there was indeed a third group involved in the drama, a group Fisher labels the "compromisers." However, what dominated Fisher's analysis was bipolarity. Perhaps the reason why the debate per se is presented in bipolar terms has to do with the extent to which bipolarity informed the entire essay. Fisher offered a useful distinction between rhetorical and dialectical activities, arguing that compromise is only possible in the former:

As [compromise] concerns the resolution of practical questions with practical proposals through persuasion, it is a rhetorical activity, not a dialectical one. Compromise is not meant to explore and to establish what is the good, the true, and the just as abstract conceptions, but to reach and implement decisions which reflect such value considerations. To the extent that theoretical questions, questions of the ultimate truth of things, can be kept from becoming paramount in debate, compromise is possible. (366)

Unfortunately, the debate Fisher examined was dialectical, not rhetorical. "Truths" were indeed at stake. And Fisher saw those "truths" in bipolar terms: "What is a slave—man or property? and What is the Constitution—compact or 'contract'?" (367). And, of course, these bipolar questions were being answered against the bipolar fact of North vs. South.

Studies after 1966 have been quite rare, but the three that exist focus on truly interesting debates. Furthermore, they suggest that much is going on that a Bakhtinian paradigm could get at more fully. Only one—my own 1997 treatment of a Senate debate over a Navy admiral's retirement rank—specifically evokes Bakhtin.

The first of the three, Vatz and Windt's 1974 essay in the *Quarterly Journal of Speech*, considered the debates over Nixon's Supreme Court nominees Haynsworth and Carswell. Although very alert to the unspoken and barely spoken dimensions of the debate, they reviewed the debate *per se* in bipolar pro vs. con terms. There were the Senators on the side of the nominees (with President Nixon sometimes in the background) and the Senators against. Vatz and Windt were much more interested in the latter side because of what they saw as this side's rhetorical dilemma. As Vatz and Windt saw the debate, the "real" argument against the nominees was tied to their conservative judicial philosophy, especially as it revealed itself on civil rights matters. That both nominees were Southerners added to this, according to Vatz and Windt, largely unexpressed concern. The forces opposed to the nominees could not make this concern explicit without risking the loss of some anti-nominee votes. So, the opposition tried to make its stand against Haynsworth on ethical grounds, arguing that he either violated ethical guidelines as a federal judge or was insufficiently concerned about maintaining the appearance of propriety. Against Carswell, the opposition did not have an ethical challenge to hide behind. Therefore, the opposition had to rely on twinned accusations of racism and incompetence.

This study is very interesting insofar as it suggests that a kind of double-voicing was occurring on the side opposed to Haynsworth and Carswell. Senators were questioning the former's judicial ethics and the latter's competence and attitude toward African Americans on the surface while raising the matter of their conservative philosophy beneath the surface. As a later chapter in this book will argue, however, this analysis is not entirely accurate. What may have misled Vatz and Windt is the bipolar paradigm that has them speaking of the opposition as a unit as opposed to many separate voices. Once the separate voices are foregrounded, the picture changes. As that later chapter will note, opposed Senators took several different approaches in rejecting the nominees. Among them was the very explicit argument against Haynsworth that the conservatism exhibited in his civil rights decisions for the Fourth Circuit disqualified him as an associate Supreme Court justice. The "hidden" argument is not hidden at all but very explicitly present in the cases offered by some of the opposed Senators. Many Senators who favored Nixon's nominees did indeed accuse the opposition of "hiding" its "real" arguments, and perhaps some members of the opposition did latch onto the arguments that the nominees were unethical or incompetent or racist because these were safer than arguments based on either their philosophy or their specific decisions on either matters of civil rights or labor-management relations. But for every opposition Senator who engaged in this kind of "double-voicing," there were two others—one arguing against the nominees for the stated reasons (ethical lapses, incompetence, racism) alone; the other arguing against the nominees for the supposedly unstated reason that their judicial philosophy was so out-of-step with the directions in which the law had moved as to be dangerously anachronistic. In addition, many Senators argued about what "advice and consent" meant and whether it was appropriate for the Senate to even consider a nominee's judicial philosophy. The debate is not only different from the way Vatz and Windt described it, but more complex.

The second of the three more recent studies is John Butler's 1995 essay in *Argumentation and Advocacy* on Illinois Senator Carol Moseley-Braun's attempt to block the use of the Confederate flag by the Daughters of the Confederacy. Butler nicely contextualized the floor debate by discussing how the Senator had unsuccessfully attempted to object during a committee hearing to Senator Orrin Hatch's questioning of Supreme Court nominee Ruth Bader Ginsburg about the reasoning in *Dred Scot v. Sanford* (1857) because Moseley-Braun, as an African American, found the discussion personally offensive. Butler perhaps understated the importance of that context when he observed that, " both of these issues surfaced on the same day and involve, as their central pressure point, the issue of race" and that, therefore, "[it] is impossible to ignore the inevitable potential of one episode informing the other in the mind of the rhetor" (62). Then, Butler examined how her refusal to accept what seemed to be defeat on the floor of the Senate led to a transformation in the manner in which members spoke. She abandoned her "lawyerly" voice and spoke from the heart as the Senate's only African American member about what the Confederate flag symbolizes. She told her colleagues that she had "tried to conform to the forum, a forum which forced her to be 'restrained and tempered'" (68). But she could not any longer—perhaps because her conforming mode of communication had led to her defeat in the committee hearing and her defeat on the Senate floor. Instead, she offered an emotional personal appeal. That appeal prompted others to share personal stories and to, in other ways, try to affiliate themselves with Moseley-Braun. The voices heard were not only different from each other but different from the Senate norm. She acted subversively and thereby evoked a rich array of voices rarely heard.

Butler's study revealed a context for her rhetorical action, described the day's drama, and analyzed the voices that her refusal to sit down evoked. A Bakhtinian perspective reveals still more of the rhetorical richness of this particular debate by describing the voices within the voices. Butler argued that the voices were different insofar as they offered narratives, celebrated how "good" it felt to join Moseley-Braun, and attempted to persuade other Senators. A Bakhtinian perspective would look even more deeply at what constituted these unusual speeches. That perspective would also consider Moseley-Braun's action as double-voiced discourse and the moment she orchestrated as "carnivalesque." Thus, a later chapter in this book extends Butler's analysis using a Bakhtinian paradigm to reveal more fully this debate's richness.

The third of the three post-1966 studies is my own 1997 *Southern Communication Journal* essay on the April 1994 debate over the retirement rank of Admiral Frank B. Kelso II. The high rank of four stars, requested by President Clinton and recommended by the Armed Services Committee, was opposed on the floor of the Senate by all seven of its female members—as well as several men—because Kelso was "in charge" at the time of the controversial "Tailhook '91" convention in Las Vegas. My approach was indeed bipolar, examining the arguments for and against the high rank. The arguments against were indeed the more interesting, and I tried to demonstrate that the speakers offering them were exhibiting a "feminine" political style and offering two sets of arguments: a "text," that being arguments directly related to Kelso's service in the Navy; and a "subtext," that being arguments related to the treatment of women in a number of patriarchal institutions, including the military, commerce, and the Congress itself. The subtext was gradually more and more noticeable as the debate proceeded.

I discussed the offering of textual and subtextual arguments in terms of Bakhtin's conception of "double-voiced discourse." There are, however, other dimensions of this debate that the prevailing bipolarity of my analysis obscured, for example, the striking differences in voices introduced into the debate by women opposed and men in favor. The women brought in the voices of victims; the men, the voices of authorities. A later chapter will use a Bakhtinian paradigm in a more thorough manner, one that discusses the debate in bipolar terms only occasionally so that the full polyphony is heard.

These two recent studies, by John Butler and myself, have escaped bipolarity somewhat by focusing much more than in the past on the many individual voices involved in a debate. Ironically, this turn takes one back to what Kirt E. Montgomery, writing in *Speech Monographs* on Thomas B. Reed of Maine, and Ralph A. Micken, writing in *Western Speech* on four Western Senators, did forty-some years ago. However, their treatments of individual debaters were heavily biographical and did not deal with the dynamics of the debates they were in. A Bakhtinian perspective would attend to the individual rhetors, to the dynamics of the communication event, and to much more. Chapter Three will describe that perspective or paradigm, situating it in Bakhtin's work.

The literature surveyed in this first chapter falls into two categories. The first category consists of attempts to assess the effects of Congressional debating. The consensus is that the effects are minimal. Thus, many of these studies attempt to ascertain why what ought to be a forum of consequence seems so much less. My position is that much of this work is wrong-headed, that analysts, for a number of reasons, have failed to appreciate the importance of Congressional debate. They have also failed to appreciate its rhetorical richness. The second category consists of the several attempts to find something rhetorically interesting in some Congressional debates. With some exceptions, this literature fails to tap the richness fully, because the analysts are imprisoned within a bipolar paradigm. This paradigm structures the way the critics think and write about these debates. As a result, there are dimensions they marginalize and questions they fail to ask. A different paradigm, one rooted in Bakhtin, would allow analysts to describe these debates more fully and thus in a manner that recognized their complexities and their nuances and thus their richness as rhetorical events.

Chapter Two

A Bakhtinian Paradigm

PRELIMINARY WORDS ON BAKHTIN

The work of Russian literary theorist Mikhail Bakhtin has alerted scholars to the multi-voiced nature of language and literature. In language, Bakhtin's key term is heteroglossia, and his key assumption is that all utterances are so contextualized that they necessarily entail other voicings. As Margaret D. Zulick notes in an essay in the *Quarterly Journal of Speech*, "Heteroglossia is a way of describing the multitude of speech genres and language styles present helter-skelter in the world" (144). We understand the world through language, and, thus, what is true of the one is by necessity true of the other. Thus, as Michael Holquist notes in *Dialogism: Bakhtin and His World* (1990), "In Bakhtin, . . . the world is a vast congeries of contesting meanings, a heteroglossia so varied that no single term capable of unifying its diversifying energies is possible" (24).

In literature, Bakhtin's key term is polyphony, and his key assumption is that the richest writing features created identities—both the people and narrators—free to voice their views to others and to themselves. "Free" suggests that the author recedes, transforming characters into people (Holquist: 162); "free" also suggests that the views may be heterodox; and "free" also suggests a form in which the voicings co-occupy space in such a way that an utterance may "belong" to one or more of the created identities. Although Bakhtin is careful to distinguish heteroglossia from polyphony, there is certainly a similarity insofar as both concepts combat simple, reductive views of human communication (Morson and Emerson: 232).

These fundamental Bakhtinian concepts, combined with a few others derived from the Russian theorist, can also combat the prevailing simple, reductive view of Congressional debating in evidence in most of the studies surveyed in the previous chapter. In fact, Bakhtin's work offers rhetorical scholars a new paradigm for considering such debates, a paradigm that leads to a more accurate description and a rhetorically richer understanding of these political communication activities. This claim would, I should note, very much surprise Bakhtin. His view of public discourse, colored by his hostility "to the monologism that Stalin and Zhdanovite apparatchiks used to organize post-revolutionary Russia under the name of 'marxism' " (Bernard-Donals, "Mikhail Bakhtin": 65) was negative. Similarly, his view of rhetoric was negative: he conceived of it as "little more than a battle between individuals, not a dialogic interchange" and, "[a]s a consequence, . . . monologic and closed" (Halasek, "Starting": 99); he followed the prevailing view of rhetoric in his day as either propagandistic or forensic (Bialostosky: 113, 115). As Bakhtin explains in "Forms of Time and Chronotope in the Novel," "Public and rhetorical forms expressing the unity of the human image had begun to ossify, had become official and conventional; heroization and glorification . . . were felt to be stereotyped and stilted. Moreover, the available public and rhetorical genres could not by their very nature provide for the expression of life that was private" (*Dialogic*: 143). He probably would have viewed legislative debates as he viewed rhetoric-filled public discourse in general. However, as Jon Klancher notes in an essay originally published in *Reclaiming Pedagogy* (1989), "A Bakhtinian pedagogy [*sic*] would show how these social languages"—that is, the ones foregrounded in the novel—"can be found and articulated within what otherwise appears as a largely univocal or 'monologic' sphere of public discourse" (24).

Bakhtin's ideas are scattered among numerous works written and sometimes re-written over decades—books such as his studies of Dostoevsky and Rabelais and the essays on the novel collected in *The Dialogic Imagination*. As James Thomas Zebroski noted in an essay originally published in the *Rhetoric Society Quarterly* in 1992, Bakhtin's output is vast; as Michael Bernard-Donals noted in an essay originally published in *College English* in 1994, that vast output offers critics an amazing diversity of analytical tools.

BAKHTIN AND THE COMMUNICATION DISCIPLINE

Several scholars, most notably Holquist in *Dialogism: Bakhtin and His World* (1990) and Morson and Emerson in *Mikhail Bakhtin: Creation of a*

Prosaics (1990), have attempted to assemble the ideas into something resembling a rhetoric or philosophy. Their work is certainly helpful in understanding Bakhtin and how his various concepts might apply to Congressional debates. Less useful but certainly suggestive are the several attempts within the communication discipline to appropriate Bakhtin for the purposes of critical analyses.

For example, several in performance studies have tried to incorporate what Holquist suggests as Bakhtin's overall idea, dialogism, into analyses of performed literature and theatre (HopKins; HopKins and Bouldin; Popovich; Conquergood, "Performance as a Moral Act"; Conquergood, "Performance and Dialogical Understanding"; Park-Fuller; Carlson). These attempts are critiqued by Bowman, who finds the Bakhtinian concept of "novelness" more useful than "dialogism." A very different appropriation, but still within performance studies, is Hoy's application of the Bakhtinian concept of the carnivalesque to English football songs.

Perhaps more directly useful are several appropriations within rhetorical criticism. Zulick ("The Agon"), for example, has used the Bakhtinian idea of polyphony to read the jeremiad, and she ("Pursuing Controversy") has pointed to the Bakhtinian concepts of double-voiced discourse and the carnivalesque as having more subversive utility than non-Bakhtinian thoughts found in Kristeva. Her suggestions are similar to those offered by literary critic Linda Hutcheon in *A Theory of Parody* (1985). Finally, Murphy has offered the Bakhtinian idea of "novelization," which he defines as "a process in which previously unquestioned discourses come to interanimate one another" (3), as a mode of discourse that embodies many of the aims of critical rhetoric while avoiding its problems. He suggests that it might be more apt to say that we live in a "novelized" world than a postmodern one, at least as post-structuralism has defined post-modernity.

Three general observations might be made about these appropriations of Bakhtinian ideas into rhetorical studies. First, they draw on many different places in Bakhtin's rambling oeuvre, suggesting its diffusiveness. As Charles I. Schuster has noted in an essay originally published in *College English* in 1985, "Although much of Bakhtin's work is considered literary criticism, his conceptions of discourse develop implications about language use in the widest possible terms" (1). These appropriations are alert to those implications. Second, each rhetorical critic seems, therefore, to be creating his or her own Bakhtin to then root her or his work in. Many have noted this phenomenon, Bernard-Donals referring to "the various Bakhtins" ("Mikhail Bakhtin": 63). As Holquist noted, "Mikhail Bakhtin made important contributions to several different areas of thought, each with its own history, its own language, and its own shared assumptions. As a result, literary scholars have perceived him as doing one sort of thing, linguists another, and anthropologists yet another" (14). Holquist argues that a comprehensive term or concept for Bakhtin is therefore lacking. David Richter, writing in 1986 in *Style*, doubts that finding such a concept is achievable, for, "there are so many of them [Bakhtin's ideas] and he reformulated them so often that no presentation could possibly be definitive" (411). Third, none of these Bakhtins seems to be precisely what is necessary from which to derive a paradigm for studying Congressional debating. Like the other critics, I'm left to create my Bakhtin.

Schuster thus referred to Bakhtin as "a kind of Zorro figure, the Masked Marvel of theoretical criticism" (1). And he was correct to a point: commentators had been in the position of constructing what was behind the mask; however, they tended to construct their Bakhtins from the same building blocks. Certain key concepts recur. Some commentators emphasize one more than another; others another more than the one. But heteroglossia, polyphony, double-voiced discourse, the carnivalesque, novelness and novelization, the chronotope, and speech genres seem to be the raw ideational material out of which the critics work. Picture Bakhtin not as Zorro but, rather, as a juggler. These concepts are the balls he juggles, and he juggles them quickly—so much so that, at times, one concept blurs into another.

BAKHTIN AND LEGISLATIVE DEBATES

Hints and ideas can be drawn from this body of work to devise a paradigm more directly applicable to the nature of legislative debates, one that puts Bakhtin's thoughts to a purpose he, a literary critic with an antipathy toward both public discourse and rhetoric, certainly never envisioned. In this chapter, I will sketch just such a paradigm, noting its roots in Bakhtin, citing both Bakhtin and commentators on Bakhtin.

The first step in such a paradigm is to get beyond the bipolar framework that has dominated the study of Congressional debates. Bakhtin may seem an odd choice to help with this step, for Bakhtin loved bipolarities. He talked in terms of centrifugal vs. centripetal forces on words, utterances, and discourse; he contrasts univocal and double-voiced discourse as well as authorized discourse and internally persuasive discourse. Although Morson and Emerson may be correct in noting the extreme bipolarity of the analysis in Bakhtin's study of Rabelais (445–46), they are incorrect when they suggest that there is a paucity of bipolar constructs elsewhere. In offering such bipolar descriptions throughout his oeuvre, Bakhtin, however, is but a product of his post-Cartesian, post-Kantian age. However, when discussing heteroglossia and polyphony, the core concepts in this critic's construction of Bakhtin, he insists on multiplicity of voicings. This insistence leads into the Bakhtinian paradigm I will present. For Bakhtin, with literature in mind, the voicings are often those of narrators or characters; however, Bakhtin makes it very clear that previous uses of words and phrases and previous users are heard in imaginative discourse. When the focus shifts from Dostoevsky and Rabelais and the novel to discourse in Congress, those voicings are those of the different Senators and Representatives and the voices they introduce by citing and quoting and the voices of previous users of words and phrases and the voices—if you will—of arguments implied, but not fully stated. All of these are included in my use of the term "voicings." A Bakhtinian paradigm suggests to critics that they ask four sets of questions in order to explore this multiplicity of voicings in Congressional debating.

First, critics of Congressional debating must get beyond the bipolarity by recognizing that there are many different voices heard, not just two sides. The critic's goal would be an accurate description. Thus, once the numerous speakers are recognized, the critic might sort their separate utterances (an utterance being bounded by a change in speaking subjects [Kent: 37]) in some manner so as to distinguish not only pro from con (if that bipolar distinction is relevant as it often partially is), but major from supporting and supporting from incidental. Knowing the degree of a given rhetor's involvement is important; so is knowing why he or she supports or rejects. The "why" may be tied to the arguments the rhetor offers or to the political context in which the arguments are made. That context would certainly, as Kay Halasek noted in an essay originally published in the *Rhetoric Society Quarterly*, include previous utterances, by the particular speaker or by others, on the subject (103). These previous voices are entailed in the voices heard in the debate per se. Also important in an accurate description would be some assessment of the fervor with which a given rhetor holds her or his position—something akin to what Bakhtin terms "tone" (Morson and Emerson: 133–34). Also important in an accurate description would be the rhetor's ideology, something the language itself, as "part and parcel of the ideological material that surrounds—and creates—human beings" (Bernard-Donals, "Mikhail Bakhtin": 66), entails. Given all of these variables, there are quite obviously many distinct voices subsumed under the usual terms "pro" and "con." An accurate description would try to validate—not lump together—all of these voices.

An accurate description would also recognize the drama of legislative debates. Although Bakhtin rejects the possibility of polyphony and drama coexisting, he is thinking of staged drama, not genuine human drama

(Bakhtin, *Problems*: 17). Staged dramas are scripted by an authorial consciousness; staged dramas are, as a result, finalizable. Human dramas are not, even when the structure imposed on them suggests an illusory finality.

Second, critics must get at the inter-voices buried beneath the words the individual legislator offers. That such voices exist is something Bakhtin insists on throughout his career. As Bakhtin notes in his study of Dostoevsky, "Our practical everyday speech is full of other people's words: with some of them we completely merge our own voice, forgetting whose they are; others, which we take as authoritative, we use to reinforce our own words; still others, finally, we populate with our own aspirations, alien or hostile to them" (*Problems*: 195). As Bakhtin notes in "From the Prehistory of Novelistic Discourse," "The forms of direct, half-hidden and completely hidden quoting were endlessly varied, as were the forms for framing quotations by a context, forms of intonational quotation marks, varying degrees of alienation or assimilation of another's quoted word" (*Dialogic:* 68).

In "Discourse in the Novel," Bakhtin repeatedly stresses the voices utterances, phrases, and words entail. I offer the following several quotations from "Discourse in the Novel" not to overwhelm (or bore) the reader, but, to emphasize how much Bakhtin stresses this idea. Note how the entailments are present whether the element of discourse be the utterance, the phrase, or the single word:

> The living utterance, having taken meaning and shape at a particular historical moment in a socially specific environment, cannot fail to brush up against thousands of living dialogic threads, woven by socio-ideological consciousness around the given object of an utterance; it cannot fail to become an active participant in social dialogue. (*Dialogic:* 276)

> In all areas of life and ideological activity, our speech is filled to overflowing with other people's words, words which are transmitted with highly varied degrees of accuracy and impartiality. (*Dialogic*: 337)

> Every conversation is full of transmissions and interpretations of other people's words. At every step one meets a "quotation" or a "reference" to something a particular person said, a reference to "people say" or "everyone says," to the words of the person one is talking with, or to one's own previous words, to a newspaper, an official decree, a document, a book, and so forth. (*Dialogic:* 338)

> [T]here are no "neutral" words and forms. . . . [L]anguage has been completely taken over, shot through with intentions and accents. (*Dialogic*: 293)

[I]n the everyday speech of any person living in society, no less than half (on the average) of all the words uttered by him will be someone else's words (consciously someone else's), transmitted with varying degrees of precision and impartiality (or more precisely, partiality). (*Dialogic*: 339)

[I]n the makeup of almost every utterance spoken by a social person—from a brief response in a casual dialogue to major verbal-ideological works (literary, scholarly, and others)—a significant number of words can be identified that are implicitly or explicitly admitted as someone else's, and that are transmitted by a variety of different means. (*Dialogic*: 354)

These inter-voices (my coinage based on the Bakhtinian term "inter-text" popularized by Julia Kristeva) are of many different sorts. In literature, inter-texts would be such things as "quotation, allusion, echo, parody, and revision" (Harmon and Holman: 274). Within Congressional debating, inter-voices would range from those of cited authorities to those of the real people who are somehow affected by the matters under discussion. Getting at them requires some kind of analytical tool if the critic is to avoid becoming lost in what Bakhtin described as "a plurality of independent and unmerged voices and consciousnesses" (*Problems*: 6). The tool should, however, be appropriate to the discourse that constitutes these debates. I would suggest that such an appropriate tool would be one that extracts the following nine types of inter-voices: (1) cited authorities; (2) quoted or paraphrased authorities; (3) what Bakhtin terms "stylization"; (4) quoted or paraphrased colleagues; (5) quoted or paraphrased self; (6) quoted or paraphrased others—perhaps constituents—who are involved, in one way or another, with the matter under discussion; (7) imagined voices; (8) the pluralized voice of those arguing together in the legislature; and (9) quoted or alluded to popular or popular culture voices. Each of these types of inter-voices requires explanation.

The first three kinds of voices are appeals to authority. In the first, the name (and perhaps the title) of the authority is all that is offered. The audience is left to imagine what words the cited authority might voice. In the second, the words are present, either directly quoted or paraphrased. As Jon Klancher noted, "Not only the quoted or paraphrased words of the third party must be figured into the dialogue, but also his or her context or motives. Further, quoting, paraphrasing, or citing introduces an explicitly hierarchical dynamic into the dialogue—the third party becomes either more or less authoritative than the writer" (26). In the third, the authority is not mentioned, but words (or even syntactic structures) associated with him or her are used. Thus, both the speaker and the unnamed authority speak; as Bakhtin puts it, the speaker stylizes her or his utterance by voicing over another's. For example, if a speaker were to support a policy by stating that it will help build a bridge into the twenty-first century, President Clinton would speak through the utterance without being explicitly named or quoted. The effect of this stylization is to lend the authority's support to the speaker's argument (Bakhtin, *Problems*: 185–91). Two historical examples of such stylization are Lyndon Johnson's use of John F. Kennedy's words in his address to a special joint session of Congress five days after Kennedy's assassination (Campbell and Jamieson: 39) and Bill Clinton's appropriation of Kennedy's language in the 1993 inaugural (Kraus: 230). Another type of stylization may be in evidence when a speaker uses the language of a lobbying or political action group. The speaker is not only bringing that group's authority to bear, but reflecting an affiliation—for good or ill—with that group. In debates today, we will often hear "lines" we associate with groups such as the National Rifle Association or pro-life and pro-choice groups. When we hear these lines, we are hearing "stylization," and it is not simply the speaker at the podium whose voice we then hear. "Lines" are easily recognized, but, as Bakhtin notes in "The Problem of Speech Genres," any utterance "reveals to us many half-concealed or completely concealed words of others with varying degrees of foreignness. Therefore, the utterance appears to be furrowed with distant and barely audible echoes " (93). Bakhtin suggests where these echoes may come from in "Discourse in the Novel":

> All words have the "taste" of a profession, a genre, a tendency, a party, a particular work, a particular person, a generation, an age group, the day and hour. Each word tastes of the context and contexts in which it has lived its socially charged life; all words and forms are populated by intentions. Contextual overtones (generic, tendentious, individualistic) are inevitable in the word. (*Dialogic*: 293)

One of the overtones may be especially important. As Morson and Emerson noted, "much of what we loosely refer to as a word's 'connotations' may in fact be the 'stylistic aura' resulting from the word's usual generic context" (294). Thus, a word or a phrase may be stylized not just by a particular previous rhetor's use (for example, Clinton, Kennedy) but also by the many rhetors who have used a given genre. This Bakhtinian concept is similar to what Karlyn Koohrs Campbell and Kathleen Hall Jamieson argue in *Deeds Done in Words* about inaugurals and other presidential speech genres: that a given speech in a well-established genre evokes many previous examples of speeches in the same genre. For example, "presidents recognize, capitalize on, and are constrained by the inaugurals of their predecessors, which, taken together, form a tradition" (21). Thus, especially memorable inaugurals—for example, Franklin Roosevelt's in 1932 or Kennedy's in 1960—return in inaugurals that follow.

With any of these three inter-voices, one needs to avoid a reductive ticking-off of the number of citations, quotations, or stylizations, although counting may be a useful initial step. Understanding how these voices are being used requires, as Klancher has noted, an awareness of the context in which and the motives with which the words were originally used. For example, when a debater stylizes by using Clinton's "bridge," with that stylization may come the exuberance of the 1996 Democratic National Convention. Or, with language that evokes John F. Kennedy's "I am a Berliner" may come the implicit firm promise of defense, regardless of cost, that motivated Kennedy's declaration. Also, a rhetor casts her or his shadow on stylizations: "the writer of prose does not meld completely with any of these words, but rather accents each of them in a particular way—humorously, ironically, parodically and so forth" (*Dialogic*: 299).

The fourth type of inter-voice may also be an appeal to authority; however, it may also be an example of the courtesy expected in legislative chambers or a gesture of political affiliation. Again, the critic needs to do more than tabulate the number of such references; the critic needs to examine the specific context, including the relationship that may exist between the rhetor speaking and the rhetor being referred to.

The fifth type—quoting or paraphrasing one's self—is not likely to be either an appeal to authority or a courtesy; rather, it is an attempt to situate one's utterance within the context of one's other discourse, perhaps to demonstrate consistency or leadership. Sometimes, introducing this inter-voice may simply be an exercise in ego-maintenance, for some members of Congress do indeed like to hear their own voices.

The sixth brings in voices often not heard in legislative debates: those of average citizens affected in one way or another by the matter under discussion. These citizens' stories are told, sometimes using their own words. Although the stories function rhetorically as evidence much as the words of authorities do, the stories also make the abstract concrete, the dead alive. These voices are especially powerful; therefore, they need to be scrutinized carefully. They entail a context and a motive; and they are accented by the rhetor when re-presented. A critic must consider both what these voices bring to the debate and how they may have been transformed in transit.

The seventh is what Classical rhetoricians termed prosopopoeia. Those affected by legislation are thereby allowed to speak fabricated words to the legislators. Or, perhaps, the legislature is given a fictive voice, and we hear what it is supposedly saying to the people. The eighth is another imagined voice, but this is the pluralized voice of those arguing together. Sometimes the pluralization is implicit in the use of "we," "us," and "our" ; at other times, the pluralization is explicitly noted. But not all pluralizations are genuinely such: some members of Congress use the editorial or royal "we," rather than "I." A notion lingers in some minds—probably based on their misunderstanding an English teacher along the way—that using "I" is improper. Some members also think that whatever they think is necessarily what others think; thus, "I" and "we" become rhetorically synonymous. So, some pluralizations are genuine attempts to embrace a community whereas others are either conventional or manifestations of sizeable Congressional egos.

The ninth inter-voice is perhaps the most difficult to define. Solemnity has so long characterized legislative bodies that references to popular culture are rare. When they are made, there is a voicing: the song's lyrics are heard; the television or movie character is heard. In the latter case, the words may be ones she or he used, or, in an example of unvoiced prosopopoeia, ones we imagine the character as probably saying. In general, in American society, the boundary between "high" culture and popular culture has become quite blurred, so politicians do invoke known voices more frequently now than in the past. Sometimes, the invoking is an attempt by the rhetor to be "cool," and the use of the inter-voice seems awkward; sometimes, the invoking seems more genuine. These voices may well be targeted at particular audiences. So, the critic needs to ask what listeners would "get" the reference and why the rhetor is being attentive to this group of listeners.

Let me emphasize that I am not suggesting that these nine inter-voices are the only possibilities; furthermore, I am not suggesting that this analytical tool is, hereafter, the way to analyze the polyphony created by the inter-voices within each speaker's discourse. I offer the tool as a first attempt to extract systematically what is within each speaker's words. I would hope that others would refine or revise the tool to improve its utility. As Bakhtin makes very apparent, the notion of voices entailing other voices is crucial to understanding human communication—be it literary or rhetorical. Therefore, the critic needs to dig deeply when executing step two.

Once these inter-voices have been extracted, a critic might look at an individual legislator's "style" of using such voices. For example, a critic might find that a given legislator cites authorities heavily whereas another tells the concrete, lived stories of "average" citizens. A critic might examine the debate as a whole and see if those rhetors in favor of a particular action introduced voices of one sort while those opposed used inter-voices of another. A critic might, in a similar manner, compare Democrats and Republicans or women and men, or—to get beyond the bipolar—legislators from different regions or of different age groups.

The third step would require scholars to look beyond the surface of this polyphony for sites of subversive double-voicing and sites of carnivalesque energy. As Bakhtin notes in "Discourse in the Novel," "Double-voiced discourse is very widespread in rhetorical genres" (*Dialogic:* 325). There are two basic types. Stylization, introduced above as a type of quoting or paraphrasing, is what Bakhtin terms "unidirectional passive double-voiced discourse." More interesting—and, thus, more frequently attended to by critics—is "varidirectional passive double-voiced discourse" (*Problems*: 194–97; Morson and Emerson: 150–54). With the latter, there is an opposing relationship between what the speaker says and what else the speaker "says," one "pulls" in one direction; the other in another. This relationship may be parodic, with the tone ranging from playful to bitter, or the opposed relationship may have the one voice speaking a tolerated argument while the other voice speaks (almost silently) the not—for whatever reason—tolerated. For example, in the debate over Haynsworth, Nixon's Supreme Court nominee, the other voice might well have been "speaking" the never-quite-there argument that the nominee's judicial philosophy was unacceptably conservative. This argument would be opposed to what Haynsworth's critics were saying, not in the sense of contradicting it but in the sense of taking the discourse in a direction other than that they purported to take it in—that is, in the direction of a discussion of the nominee's ethics. Although, as I suggested earlier, Vatz and Windt do not describe the double-voicing in the Haynsworth debate with complete accuracy, they are quite alert to this and other possible double-voicings in their analysis of this debate. However, they lacked the Bakhtinian framework that ellucidates the multiply-directed "pulls" of an utterance. To discern these rhetorical dynamics, the critic must get beyond the surface of the text with an adequate critical lexicon. This step is crucial, for what goes on beyond that surface may well be some of the most politically interesting communication. The dynamics are not necessarily simple, although they do, according to Bakhtin, tend to be simpler in rhetorical discourse than in literature. As he notes in "Discourse in the Novel," "[I]n most cases the double-voicedness of rhetoric is abstract and lends itself to formal, purely logical analysis of the ideas that are parceled out in voices" (*Dialogic*: 354). In other words, we are more likely to be able to critique varidirectional, passive double-voiced discourse in rhetorical communication (as opposed to in literature) in terms such as "opposed" or "parodic" or "differently directed."

In *Problems of Dostoevsky's Poetics*, Bakhtin offers a scheme for analyzing discourse referred to above: as Morson and Emerson note, "for Bakhtin elaborate classifications were a mental habit" (392). It is this scheme that gives us the distinctions between single-voiced and double-voiced, between unidirectional and varidirectional, between active and passive. Of all of the possibilities Bakhtin charts (literally charts), the most interesting rhetorically is passive varidirectional double-voiced discourse because of its ability to introduce positions into an argument that subvert authority without overtly disrupting the argument (Morson and Emerson: 146–59, 199). For example, if on a medical matter, one group of rhetors argued using heavily statistical, jargon-infested studies as evidence, an opposing group might counter with similar evidence. On one level, the counter evidence would serve as refutation; on another level, the counter evidence could be parodic and suggest that the initial group's reliance on such studies reflects its refusal—and perhaps the dominant culture's refusal—to deal with the medical matter in a human manner that recognizes that people and their bodies are at stake. The double-voicing would take the argument in a direction other than the one apparent in the exchange of evidence. That direction would subvert both the argument and the prevailing culture that treats the argument as normative. The subversion, in this case, would be "intended" by the opposing rhetors; thus, the parodic second level would be "passive," that is, it would not have a life of its own beyond the rhetor's control.

Bakhtin's recognition of the subversive potential of passive varidirectional double-voiced discourse is, I think, what motivated him to merge a discussion of the carnivalesque into the revised edition of his study of Dostoevsky in 1963. Bakhtin saw how two ideas, derived from different parts of his oeuvre, were consonant. I should note that not all commentators on Bakhtin see this consonance. Morson and Emerson, for example, say, "In reading the new chapter four [in the Dostoevsky study], therefore, we must ask ourselves how organic its discussion of carnival and menippean satire is to the structure and logic of the book as a whole" (458). Their answer is that the discussion is not organic; furthermore, they argue that "the revised Dostoevsky book amends the concept of carnival so that it can be combined with that of dialogue" (469). I think Morson and Emerson (and others) are guilty of misreading Bakhtin's discussion of the carnivalesque in Rabelais as suggesting what the carnivalesque must always be. Rather, Bakhtin offers in *Rabelais and His World* one example of what that energy is. What he says in the revised Dostoevsky book suggests that there is a range of discourse types that exhibit carnivalesque energy, some more raucous than others and some more subversive of prevailing hierarchies than others. As Bernard-Donals notes, in the several attempts to summarize Bakhtin, "Something is always left out . . . or glossed over" ("Mikhail Bakhtin": 63–64). The relegation of the carnivalesque to the final chapter in Morson and Emerson's *Mikhail Bakhtin: Creation of a Prosaics* suggests that this is the concept that they are having a difficult time fitting into their summary.

That last chapter, however, is not without merit, for, in it, Morson and Emerson establish quite well that the idea of the "carnivalesque" was a fluid concept in Bakhtin's writings (433). Its fluidity makes it one of the trickiest to use. Bakhtin seems to recognize at least three possible uses of the concept; furthermore, he does not consistently privilege any one of them. The first is the folk use, as in the medieval carnival (and perhaps the Trinidadian carnival). The second is literary, but in forms largely unlicensed, such as Rabelais' "Menippean" satires (Bakhtin, *Rabelais*: 246, 251). The third is also literary, but in forms that are more culturally approved (Bakhtin, *Problems*: 123).

The degree of irreverence varies as one might expect as one moves through the three uses, so much so that the last is associated in Bakhtin's oeuvre with the concept of "reduced laughter." It is worth noting, however, that the degree of irreverence may well be somewhat controlled in all three cases. Even in the first case, as Morson and Emerson note, the carnivalesque impulse was regulated: "Church and state authorities tolerated and integrated it, set aside special days when exiled laughter could be celebrated, and thus 'licensed' carnival even as they regulated its scope" (455). Hoy, in summarizing Linda Hutcheon's explication of Bakhtin in *A Theory of Parody*, raises the question more fully:

In her work on Bakhtin Linda Hutcheon has pointed out that there is something quite ironic about the fact that the carnivalesque involves rigid regularities, discrete groups, graduated hierarchies and so on, which brings up the question of just how carnivalesque this kind of structured, rigorous, hierarchical festivity really is. . . . It could possibly be argued that . . . the idea of carnival [is] a safety valve, with an essentially conservative function socially. It would be unwise to forget that the potential of carnival for radical rebellion is in the end politically limited, since it is, after all, licensed misrule, a contained and officially sanctioned rebellion, after which everybody gets back to work. (291)

So, the carnivalesque may only seem more radical in the cases of the folk carnival and Rabelais than in more valorized literature. If so, then the supposed revision of the concept so that it fits into the revised Dostoevsky study is not as dramatic as Morson and Emerson suggest.

Here, I need to take a detour into Bakhtin for a minute—to bring together several Bakhtinian threads that are being pulled by different rhetorical critics in different ways. Bakhtin, I would guess, probably conceived of his work on the carnivalesque, his work on polyphony and its best exemplar Dostoevsky, and his work on the history and anatomy of the novel as separate projects. Not surprisingly, however, he was asking a similar question in all three: how do the voices of human (social) life, especially those subversive of any and all hegemonic forces, emerge in literary discourse? The answers he arrived at in the three projects were, in my judgment, really the same essential answer. The voices, there in a raw form in carnival, find their way into satire, especially the raucous type penned by Rabelais. The voices, there in any real life social scene, find their way into the polyphony of Dostoevsky because he allowed the consciousnesses he created to express themselves freely and interact freely as in a real life social scene. Voices, there in genres that defy or exist despite or thrive beneath that which is authorized (and, thus, univocal), find their way into discourse that is fully novelized (Morson and Emerson: 258). In addition, every fictive person's previous comments are entailed when he or she speaks; furthermore, many previous authors' words are entailed when a given author writes (Morson and Emerson: 337, 347). Thus, as Holquist notes, "Novels are overwhelmingly intertextual" referring to "the enormous variety of discourses used in different historical periods by disparate social classes," not just novels per se (88). The "mix" of voices and languages in the novel and other novelized genres is described by Bakhtin in the following terms:

A third characteristic is the deliberate multi-styled and hetero-voiced nature of all these genres. They reject the stylistic unity (or better, the single-styled nature) of the epic, the tragedy, high rhetoric, the lyric. Characteristic of these genres are a multi-toned narration, the mixing of high and low, serious and comic; they make wide use of inserted genres—letters, found manuscripts, retold dialogues, parodies on the high genres, parodically reinterpreted citations; in some of them we observe a mixing of prosaic and poetic speech, living dialects and jargon (and in the Roman stage, direct bilingualism as well) are introduced, and various authorial masks make their appearance. Alongside the representing word there appears the *represented* word; in certain genres a leading role is played by the double-voiced word. And what appears here, as a result, is a radically new relationship to the word as the material of literature. (*Problems:* 108)

This richness results in the novel being "the most accurate conceptualization of human experience ever developed," "[t]he greatest of [the] disharmonious genres," "ever skeptical, experimental, and open to the unpredictable experience of every present moment," and "not just a complex form of thinking, but . . . also the supreme achievement of Western thought, greater than all other genres as well as all schools of philosophy" (Morson and Emerson: 280, 300, 303, 307–8). As Bakhtin puts it in his essay "Epic and Novel," "The novel has become the leading hero in the drama of literary development in our time precisely because it best of all reflects the tendencies of a new world still in the making" (*Dialogic:* 7).

Whether the focus be carnival, polyphony, or the novel, the answer to the question has much the same ring (if not the same number of laudatory appositives). That these answers are so similar explains, I think, some of the revising Bakhtin did late in his career—most notably the introduction of the carnivalesque and the history of the novel genre in Chapter Four of the revised Dostoevsky book. Once a critic recognizes that these once disparate Bakhtinian concepts are merging late in the theorist's oeuvre, the critic begins to see the carnivalesque, polyphony, and novelization as being different faces of the same communication phenomenon. Envision it as a pyramid, if you will. The faces represent the three energetic impulses; the base represents their merger. Discourse can be mapped anywhere onto this pyramid, as well as "off" the pyramid if it lacks energy and is hegemonic and univocal.

Congressional debating, as discourse, can be similarly mapped. The procedure I am introducing here is designed to accomplish such a mapping. Sometimes, the debate under analysis will fall on a face; sometimes on the base. Thus, the concepts and terms polyphony, carnivalesque, and novelization will vary in their applicability. A debate with many voices will be described as polyphonic; a debate featuring subversion as carnivalesque; a debate featuring genres other than the usual "remarks" as novelized. And a debate could feature many voices, subversion, and unauthorized genres and be polyphonic, carnivalesque, and novelized. A debate could also be "off" the pyramid entirely, in which case it would probably not be an especially rich case to examine. But whichever way the analysis goes, it is getting at the same essential communication phenomenon—how the energy and humanness of utterances and the words that comprise them find their way into all but the most sterile, most univocal discourse.

The carnivalesque, then, is but one way in which the energy and humanness may manifest itself, but it is not a simple, single entity. What I would call the carnivalesque continuum is important to note, for one can err if one expects all that exhibits the carnivalesque to be as raw as the folk carnival. What unifies these many manifestations is not the scatological or bawdy but rather the subversion of authority and, thereby, "the suspension of all hierarchic differences, of all ranks and status," for "[i]n the world of carnival all hierarchies are canceled" (Bakhtin, *Rabelais*: 246, 251). Bakhtin's formulation—in both the study of Rabelais and in the revised study of Dostoevsky—of the carnivalesque stressed how hierarchical relationships are subverted:

> The laws, prohibitions, and restrictions that determine the structure and order of ordinary, that is noncarnival, life are suspended during carnival: what is suspended first of all is hierarchical structure and all the forms of terror, reverence, piety, and etiquette connected with it—that is, everything resulting from socio-hierarchical inequality or any other form of inequality among people (including age). All distance between people is suspended. . . . People who in life are separated by impenetrable hierarchical barriers enter into free familiar contact on the carnival square. . . . Carnival is the place for working out, in a concretely sensuous, half-real and half-play-acted form, a new mode of interrelationship between individuals, counterpoised to the all-powerful socio-hierarchical relationships of noncarnival life. (*Problems*: 122–23)

And, as Bakhtin sees it, discourse can be carnivalesque and subversive even if couched in forms that are culturally approved. Bakhtin seems to recognize that there can be, within valorized forms of discourse, the rhetorical equivalents of the folk carnival's irreverence and celebration, thereby "relativizing all that was externally stable, set, and ready-made" (Bakhtin, *Problems*: 166). In Congress, those equivalents can well be part of a debate—especially once those historically disempowered by the dominant culture acquire the ability to act rhetorically in an arena still regulated by that culture.

Bakhtin and commentators on Bakhtin stress how the carnivalesque emerges from beneath, from the disempowered. As Zulick notes, it is "a moment of destruction, a clearing away of ossified social forms in time, and always from below, thus fixing the possibility of revolt in the social" ("Pursuing": 99). This possibility makes this particular Bakhtinian notion—along with double-voiced discourse—especially appealing to "feminist" critics. At least two of my case studies in the chapters that follow demonstrate that there is much to be gleaned in these bits of Bakhtin by "feminist" rhetors or "feminist" critics. But the use of Bakhtin by "feminist" critics is not without difficulty, for, as Kay Halasek has noted in an essay originally published in the *Rhetoric Society Quarterly*, Bakhtin does not even mention gender. In appropriating Bakhtin into "feminist" criticism, Halasek follows Julia Kristeva and Dale Bauer:

> [T]he concept of "carnival"—necessary rebellion and subversion—corroborates a feminist agenda of social, linguistic, and political rebellion. In adapting Bakhtin's work to feminist ends, Kristeva allies feminism with carnivalistic and subversive linguistic tendencies. . . . Dale Bauer extends Kristeva's commentary. ("Feminism": 55)

Women and other historically disempowered groups thus can enact the carnivalesque. And, although this observation will be shown true in the case studies that follow, one must note that, within the political context, even the empowered may in certain contexts be the disempowered. As the analysis of the poll tax debate in Chapter Six will demonstrate, in the civil rights debates of the 1960s, many Southerners felt disempowered by the rush of events and the legislation that were questioning their way of life and their states' rights. Thus, although many were very powerful figures on Capitol Hill, they could be the disempowered in the context of certain debates and could exhibit the carnivalesque within those contexts.

The fourth step in the Bakhtinian paradigm requires scholars to recognize the illusory nature of the finalizability implicit in the vote that concludes the debates and to look beyond this vote. Craig A. Smith in *Political Communication* (1990) discusses the several roles that legislative debates serve (145–47). Although the arguments offered during such debates are voiced in order to sway some votes, the speakers usually are looking more to the future than at the present. Since the actual vote is more often than not already known, the speakers are looking toward future debates, toward future elections. Smith is correct to note this future orientation; however, he still views the debate as finalizable and, thus, these futures as outside the debate, as other events. If Bakhtin's insistence on polyphony's absence of finalizability—what Morson and Emerson term "an all-purpose carrier of his conviction that the world is not only a messy place, but an open place" (36)—were superimposed on Smith's discussion, then these futures become neither outside nor other but essential to the continuing dialogue. Although Smith removes these futures from the category of footnotes by stressing their importance, a Bakhtinian perspective removes them still farther by insisting on their being essential. A Bakhtinian perspective, then, rejects the debate as finalizable and thereby integrates these futures into an account of the communication event. A similar distinction (but not one explicitly rooted in Bakhtin) is offered by Jansinski in his account of Henry Clay's "rhetorical restraint" in 1850–51, which separated immediate issues, which could be resolved, from forensic and epideictic issues that would be part of an ongoing debate.

SUMMARY

One of the more "memorable" features of Bakhtin's critical writings is the chart in the Dostoevsky book on which he presents the various types of discourse that constitute heteroglossia. In the spirit of that chart, let me conclude this chapter by offering a chart of my own that attempts to outline, in brief, the paradigm this book is suggesting.

Step 1—Identify who all the speakers are

distinguish between pro and con (if dichotomy is relevant);

distinguish major from supporting and incidental;

ask why do speakers speak—is the answer tied to their ideas, their political context, or both;

pinpoint to what extent previous utterances (by the speakers themselves or by others) are embedded in the political context;

identify the degree of fervor or "tone" for the various speakers;

identify the ideology implicit in the various speakers' utterances;

describe the dramatic structure of the debate (while remembering that it is not finalizable, as a crafted drama would be).

Step 2—Identify inter-voices

pinpoint citations to or references to authorities;

pinpoint quoted or paraphrased words:

consider context in which words were originally spoken;

consider original speaker's motives;

identify hierarchical relationship between speaker and quoted speaker;

pinpoint stylizations:

look for the words and phrases of other speakers;

look for the words and phrases of lobbying or political action groups;

identify to what extent the words and phrases are evoked to
lend authority or to establish affiliation;

for imported words, look for entailments of profession, political party, generation/age group, or genre;

identify original context and motives;

identify how speaker has accented imported words and phrases;

pinpoint references to colleagues' words:

ask if the references are a courtesy, or is speaker invoking
authority or establishing affiliation;

pinpoint references to speaker's own previous words:

ask if references are a way to situate oneself (for example,
as leader), a demonstration of consistency, or a manifestation of ego;

pinpoint the voices of constituents or those in some way affected
by or involved in the matters under discussion:

identify these other speakers' original motives and contexts;

identify how the speaker accents these imported voices;

pinpoint examples of prosopopoeia, noting whose fictive voice
is being presented;

pinpoint pluralizations:

ask if they are genuine or conventional;

ask if they are attempts to embrace a community or manifest one's ego;

pinpoint popular culture "voices":

ask if they are contrived or genuine;

identify what constituency groups these "voices" seem an
appeal to;

ask if particular legislators have a "style" of using inter-voices;

look for interesting contrasts—for example between political
parties, between genders, among regions.

Step Three—Identify any double-voiced discourse (varidirectional,
passive) or evocations of carnivalesque energy

if former, specify how the voices are related (for example,
parodic, allowed vs. disallowed, differently directed);

if latter, specify what hierarchies are being challenged.

Step Four—Go beyond the debate per se

> ask how debate relates to events—particular other rhetorical events—that preceded it in time;
>
> ask how debate relates to events—particular other rhetorical events—that followed it in time.

Again, in the spirit of Bakhtin, let me emphasize that this paradigm lacks finalizability. I would be contradicting "the master" if I suggested otherwise. But more importantly, I would be pretending that I am doing something more in this chapter and in the case studies that follow than initiating a dialogue on how Bakhtin's ideas can invigorate the study of Congressional debating. I am convinced that the Bakhtinian paradigm "charted" above leads to a fuller description of these debates, one attentive to nuances commentators have largely neglected. I am also convinced that the paradigm reveals much more of their complexity and, therefore, their rhetorical richness—more than the "old" paradigm that is limited by its bipolarity and an implicitly negative attitude (or at least an apologetic attitude) toward the subject being studied. I am not convinced, however, that the paradigm, as I have outlined it, is yet the Bakhtinian approach. It is, rather, much more of an initial utterance.

I am obviously talking about political communication in the legislature now in terms that are both different and—for the moment—abstract. What I would like to do in the six chapters that follow is make this approach concrete by applying it to particular debates in the United States Congress. To establish the validity and superiority of this new paradigm will, of course, require many more applications. I cannot make that full case here. What I hope these particular applications will show is, first, how one might apply the paradigm, and, second, what the paradigm might reveal about a kind of political communication often misanalyzed—reductively analyzed—because of the imprisoning effects of bipolar assumptions—and often underrated. What I have outlined above as a four-step procedure is heuristic. One's written analysis would focus on what such a procedure revealed. Because my purpose is as much to illustrate the paradigm's use as to illuminate these particular debates, I will foreground the procedure more than would ordinarily be the case in a critical essay. Nonetheless, one should not expect, even in these cases, a rigid following of the questions outlined above. The questions serve as a heuristic device to get at what is interesting, from a communication perspective, in each debate. What one does then, after considering many of the listed questions in my chart, is weave them into an analysis, a reading. The cases do that, sometimes emphasizing some matters; sometimes others. Certain questions seem crucial—for example, how inter-voices are used; other questions are provocative but not yet as fully operationalized as they might be—for example, how entailments of profession, party, generation, or group constitute stylizations and therefore voice and intrude a group's (perhaps an elite group's) power into a debate. That these other questions are not fully operationalized is, perhaps, a limitation of the case studies. Rather, I prefer to think of these questions as having a pregnant liminality that others who embrace and refine this paradigm will bring to life more than I have. As I've said, a Bakhtinian paradigm should refuse finalizability because Bakhtin rejected finalizability.

Chapter Three

Carol Moseley-Braun Defies the Confederate Flag

On July 22, 1993, Senator Carol Moseley-Braun of Illinois hurried to the Senate Chamber to, as she put it, kill Dracula again (S 9258). She had thought that she (and others) had put to rest the Daughters of the Confederacy's request for a renewal of their patented use of the Confederate Flag during Judiciary Committee hearings. However, Senators Jesse Helms and Strom Thurmond, believing that the Committee's action was a slap in the face of the Daughters of the Confederacy, brought the issue to the floor via an amendment to an unrelated piece of education legislation (S 9251–71).

VOICES

Helms and Thurmond spoke; Moseley-Braun (joined briefly by Senators Howard Metzenbaum and Patty Murray) spoke. Then, there was a vote, against tabling the motion granting the patent. Moseley-Braun, upset by this vote, refused to yield the floor until the Senate changed its mind. Several rallied to her side, including members who had voted against tabling. So, after what Butler correctly discusses as an unusually emotional sharing of personal histories by members of the Senate, the Senate reconsidered the matter and tabled the motion, in essence denying the patent. Before and after that vote, many thanked Moseley-Braun for what she had brought, as an African American, to the Senate that day. Only Helms refused to join in the celebration, characterizing the comments against the patent as "political rhetoric and partisan oratory," the racism issue as "a political ploy," and his colleagues as "pious, self-satisfied Senators" and "turncoats who ran for cover for political reasons" (S 9271). Thus, conflict led to a defeat, which created tension. The tension then led to a catharsis, which then led to victory and celebration—a dramatic structure reminiscent of Shakespearean comedy—except for one Jacques-like bitter voice, one who, in this case, responded to events by saying, "I felt that I was going to throw up" (S 9271).

INTER-VOICES

This drama, as Butler notes, is compelling. What is perhaps more interesting is the change in the use of inter-voices that occurs as one moves through the drama. Helms and Thurmond mixed references to authorities with stories of the service the Daughters of the Confederacy have performed. In telling his colleagues the history of the organization, Helms evoked the authority of past presidents:

> In the years following the War Between the States, thousands of men and women came together in reunions across the country. They buried the sword, and they paid honor to each other. It was in this spirit that Congress and Presidents Arthur, Cleveland, Harrison, and McKinley—the last two being former Union soldiers—encouraged the formation of groups such as the United Daughters of the Confederacy, not to refight the battles long since lost, but to preserve the memory of courageous men who fought and died for the [cause] they believed in. (S 9251)

Helms cited authorities from the previous century; Thurmond, on the other hand, focused on what Congress has "said" by its actions in the twentieth century:

> This amendment is essentially the same language which we approved last year to extend and renew the design patent for the insignia of the United Daughters of the Confederacy. This design patent was originally issued on November 8, 1898 and has been extended on numerous occasions since then. It was extended in 1926, 1941, 1963, and 1977. In November of last year the patent expired. In order to ensure continued protection for the insignia, Congress must extend design patent protection for the UDC. (S 9252)

Thurmond later noted how Congress had honored similar groups, again bringing the voice of previous Congressional action to bear on the amendment he had cosponsored:

Mr. President, for the record, I want to note recognition granted by the Congress to several other groups whose origin can be traced to the Civil War. The Congress has granted Federal Charters to the Ladies of the Grand Army of the Republic, the Sons of Union Veterans of the Civil War, the National Women's Relief Groups, Auxiliary to the Grand Army of the Republic, and the Daughters of Union Veterans of the Civil War. Additionally, most of these groups have been granted by the Congress exclusive rights to the use of their name, emblem, seals, and badges. (S 9253)

Together with citations of what previous Presidents and previous Congresses did and thereby "said," Thurmond and Helms talked about the United Daughters of the Confederacy (UDC). Helms talked about the group's service during World War II:

During World War II, the United Daughters of the Confederacy continued to offer its services to the U.S. Government for war relief. They provided financial support, donated ambulances, established a blood plasma unit, sold millions of dollars in war bonds and were ultimately recognized by the War Department and the Red Cross for its outstanding work and contributions. (S 9252)

Helms zeroed in on the story of Oveta Culp Hobby:

In World War II, the UDC answered Franklin Roosevelt's summons by sponsoring the Nurse Cadet Corps, by raising money for war bonds, and by organizing blood plasma drives. The head of the Texas chapter, Oveta Culp Hobby, was asked by the Chief of Staff of the Army, Gen. George C. Marshall, to draw up the plans for the establishment of the Women's Army Corps, known to history as the WAC's. And this same Oveta Culp Hobby was the first Secretary of Health, Education, and Welfare under President Eisenhower. This lady, as I said, was president of the Texas chapter of the UDC. (S 9252)

Helms and Thurmond offered a mixture of evidence types—authorities and narratives, which evoked the persona of the folksy Southern lawyer.

Helms' sole use of prosopopoeia had this same flavor: "It [a rejection of the patent renewal] will be rewriting history to say to them, 'you no longer count, and you no longer are going to have a recognition that so many other organizations have had since the turn of the century—including the UDC' " (S 9252).

Moseley-Braun used a style she herself termed "lawyerly" (S 9257). It lacked the folksiness of Helms' and Thurmond's in its mixture of common knowledge and cited and quoted authorities. It is very legalistic, very rational. She talked about the symbolism of the Confederate flag in a restrained tone:

> The fact of the matter is the emblems of the Confederacy have meaning to Americans even 100 years after the end of the Civil War. Everybody knows what the Confederacy stands for. Everybody knows what the insignia means. That matter of common knowledge is not a surprise to any of us. When a former Governor stood and raised the Confederate battle flag over the Alabama State Capitol to protest the Federal Government support for civil rights and a visit by the Attorney General at the time in 1963, everybody knew what that meant. (S 9254)

One can "feel" Senator Moseley-Braun holding back. Similarly, as she introduced and then discussed a letter she received from Michael K. Kirk, Acting Assistant Secretary of the U.S. Commerce Department and Acting Commissioner of Patents and Trademarks, one can hear the lawyer in her. The following quotations are excerpts from the words she used while presenting her evidence:

> Mr. President, I will have printed in the RECORD a letter to me dated April 30, 1993, from Mr. Kirk, of the U.S. Department of Commerce, Patents and Trademarks Office.

> Mr. President, he answered this question: Is it common practice for nonprofit groups to obtain design patents for their insignia and logos?

> In other words, what he is saying is that most organizations have other kinds of protections and do not have this design patent, which is sought today by the United Daughters of the Confederacy.

> The next question asked in the letter is: Are design patents typically renewed?

This is more than a second renewal for this organization. It is not necessary to begin with. They can continue to use their insignia. It does not interfere with their charitable activities. (S 9254)

After the initial vote, Moseley-Braun's inter-voices and her tone changed. She "announced" that change:

Madam President, I really had not wanted to have to do this because in my remarks I believe that I was restrained and tempered. I talked about the committee procedure. I talked about the lack of germaneness of this amendment. I talked about how it was not necessary for this organization to receive the design patent designation, which was an extraordinary extension of an extraordinary act to begin with. What I did not talk about and what I am constrained now to talk about with no small degree of emotion is the symbolism. (S 9256–57)

She described her earlier tone as "dispassionate" and "lawyering about" (S 9257); now, she will, with emotions that she occasionally feels obliged to apologize for, tell how the Confederate flag symbolizes "the single most painful episode in American history" (S 9257) from the perspective of African Americans. She speaks, in personal terms, of how African Americans see the flag and the vote that just occurred:

I am sorry, Madam President. I will lower my voice. I am getting excited, because, quite frankly, that is the very issue. The issue is whether or not Americans, such as myself, who believe in the promise of this country, who feel strongly and who are patriots in this country, will have to suffer the indignity of being reminded time and time again, that at one point in this country's history we were human chattel. We were property. We could be traded, bought, and sold.
    It is an outrage. It is an insult. It is absolutely unacceptable to me and to millions of Americans, black or white, that we would put the imprimatur of the United States Senate on a symbol of this kind of idea. (S 9257)

She very emotionally tried to tell her colleagues what it is like to be an African American and what it is like to be an (the only) African American in the Senate. She also evoked popular culture, personifying the patent design request several times as Dracula. She also heavily used prosopopoeia. She gave voice to how the American voters responded to the 1992 Republican

National Convention: "Folks took a look at the convention and said, my God, what are these people standing for? This is not America" (S 9257). She imagined the voice of those who voted against tabling the Helms amendment: " 'Well, we are just going to do this, you know, because it is no big deal' " (S 9258).

As others joined her, we heard more prosopopoeia, more stories, and many networking references to Moseley-Braun and the others who were joining her cause. Both the stories and the affiliative references to Moseley-Braun are worth examining closely.

As Butler notes, the stories—and the emotional way they are told—are quite striking because they are atypical of discourse in the usually staid Senate. After she told her story and that of her ancestors, Native American Senator Ben Lighthorse Campbell told his. He first identified himself as "the only other so-called person of color" in the Senate. He then spoke about places in the United States where his Native American people are "called prairie niggers" and of how one VFW representative tried to block a chapter's endorsement of Campbell, a veteran of the Korean War, because he was an Indian. He noted how Southern Senators were citing "tradition" in defense of the UDC and the Confederate flag and stated that, "slavery was once a tradition, like killing Indians like animals was once a tradition. That did not make them right" (S 9261).

Then, Senator Howell Heflin of Alabama offered his story. He talked about his Southern roots:

> I come from a family background that is deeply rooted in the Confederacy. My great-grandfather on my mother's side was one of the signers of the Ordinance of Secession by which the State of Alabama seceded from the Union. My grandfather on my father's side was a surgeon in the Confederate Army.
>
> I have many connections through my family with the Daughters of the Confederacy organization and the Children of the Confederacy, and I have a deep feeling, relative to my family's background, that what they did at the time they thought was right. (S 9262)

He then noted that "we live today in a different world," "in a Nation that everyday is trying to heal the scars of racism" (S 9262). He cited a conversation that he had with his Black legislative director: they, somewhat jokingly, compared notes on how their buried ancestors would react to the stands the Senator might take. Heflin concluded that his ancestors would, if alive in 1993, "stand for what is right and honorable"; therefore, Heflin decided to change his vote and, when the matter was reconsidered, voted to table the Helms amendment.

Campbell and Heflin shared their personal stories in announcing their support for the position Moseley-Braun had staked out. Senator Mitch McConnell from Kentucky shared his story to explain his vote against Moseley-Braun:

My roots, like the senior Senator from Alabama, run deep in the South. . . . My great grandmother's first husband was killed in the Civil War. I have learned that he was not a slaveholder, but he, like others in Alabama, viewed that conflict through the lenses of those days. And his view was that it was a fight for his region. My grandmother belonged to the United Daughters of the Confederacy. I know she did not support slavery. So it has been my view in growing up that the UDC largely was a group not about the purpose of glorifying slavery, but a group that very much revered the lives of those who were lost during that great conflict. (S 9264)

McConnell, "out of respect for [his] ancestors," (S 9264) decided to vote to support the UDC's request. He did, however, very much want his colleagues to understand how his personal story had led him to his vote.

References to Moseley-Braun's words are understandably numerous in the speeches Senators made while she is defiantly maintaining control of the floor in the wake of the 48–52 vote not to table the Helms amendment. Let me quote some of these references:

FEINSTEIN: So I would like to submit to you, Madam President, that Senator Carol Moseley-Braun is correct. Carol, I think you said it the way it had to be said. You said it eloquently. You said it beautifully. (S 9258)

BRADLEY: I appeal to people who voted for this amendment to understand not just the wisdom, but the passion and the depth of feeling from which Senator Moseley-Braun spoke. (S 9258)

MOYNIHAN: May I say to the distinguished Senator from Illinois that in my 17 years in this body, I have been not so moved as by her statement. (S 9260)

BIDEN: [M]y whole purpose here in going through this charade is to compliment the Senator. (S 9261)

SIMON: Mr. President, I simply want to tell my colleague from Illinois how proud I am of her at this moment. (S 9264)

RIEGLE: First of all, I want to say to the Senator from Illinois how I appreciate her extraordinary leadership today. (S 9264)

BOXER: To the Senator from Illinois, I thank her for guiding us, for teaching us, for reminding us, for being insistent, for standing on her feet, for appealing to what is best in us. (S 9266)

CONRAD: Mr. President, the statement of the Senator from Illinois, Carol Moseley-Braun, I think, was perhaps the most powerful, most moving statement I have heard on the floor of the Senate since I came here 7 years ago. (S 9266)

METZENBAUM: Mr. President, I rise because I have seen something here today that I have not seen since I have been in the Senate. I saw one person, who was able to make a difference, stand up and fight for what she believes in, and she gave a message to this body that electrified the body. (S 9266)

KENNEDY: Mr. President, the Senator from Illinois, like another great leader from Illinois, President Lincoln, appealed to the better angels in us this afternoon. She reminded us in a most eloquent way about the wounds, torn in the fabric of our society as a result of the Civil War and racism, that still exist. (S 9266)

MITCHELL: The eloquence, the conviction, the power of the remarks made by the Senator from Illinois, the persuasiveness as seen in the subsequent remarks, is something rarely seen in the Senate. (S 9267)

LAUTENBERG: Madam President, I have been here 10 years now, and there have been few, if any, occasions in which the remarks of a U.S. Senator left the kind of impression that the comments made by Senator Moseley-Braun, of Illinois, have made because she touched the nerve of everybody who had the opportunity to hear what she was saying. (S 9270)

DODD: I just want to join with others in commending the distinguished junior Senator from Illinois. This was a truly remarkable moment. She gave a wonderful speech. (S 9270)

DOUBLE-VOICING AND CARNIVALESQUE

Moseley-Braun's words created a network on July 22, 1993. She wove together an affiliation of Senators who wished not only to share her commitment to racial justice but also the emotion and the honesty with which she expressed herself. Her creating such an affiliation centered on not just an idea but on a manner of speaking contrary to the somewhat somber tradition of the Senate. This manner set the stage for the carnivalesque.

Eventually joined by these many others, Moseley-Braun effects carnivalesque subversion. The Senate is a place wrapped in its rules and its courtesies. After the initial vote, the two clashed. Although Moseley-Braun had no right to the floor, she took it and refused to yield it. Her peers, out of courtesy, did not try to have her declared out of order; rather, they—after some prodding by Moynihan—listened to what she had to say. As she held the floor (speaking to business already concluded), her allies gathered, and, working with some Senators who had initially voted against Moseley-Braun, they constructed a motion to reconsider. That motion eventually is introduced: all the while, Moseley-Braun is speaking, yielding time she had no right to have to others for questions that were really statements.

If it were not for the seriousness of the issue under discussion, the way the procedure unfolded would be almost comic. Moseley-Braun declared, "I will do everything I can to see to it that this body does not disgrace itself by giving its imprimatur to a symbol of a flag that was defeated in the Civil War" (S 9260). Determined "to take this floor and not give it up forever" (S 9269) and committed to "stand[ing] here until this room freezes over" (S 9258), Moseley-Braun yielded to a succession of colleagues. Bradley, after his statement, said, "So I am getting to my question" (S 9259). Exon began his statement by saying, "I will ask a question in just a moment" (S 9259). Campbell referred to the unusual "convention" that was being practiced and said "I will be getting around to my question in a short time" (S 9261). Biden, when it was finally time for a question after his long statement, said, "So my question to the Senator is one I cannot think of because my whole purpose here in going through this charade is to compliment the Senator" (S 9261). He did eventually think of a question, but, like the previous questions, it was part of a veil that allowed colleagues to speak—usually in support—while Moseley-Braun maintained control of the floor, something she really had no right to do. As this serious, emotional, but nonetheless comic "debate" ensued, Moseley-Braun stood in the well—conducting what amounted to a single-handed filibuster.

The discussion did not proceed as it should have. Moseley-Braun subverted procedures, and, in the carnivalesque energy her subversion created, the Senate regrouped, increasingly showing solidarity around her. During the regrouping, the Senators spoke differently, and, after it, they voted differently. During the carnivalesque moment, Moseley-Braun brought the body into the discourse in two ways that were subversive. First, she brought in the bodies of her slave ancestors—bodies that were bought and sold like livestock. Second, she kept her body—the only African American body in the U.S. Senate—before her peers by refusing to yield the floor. No matter who spoke, Senator Moseley-Braun physically was center stage. I emphasize the body at this point for a reason. Bakhtin's discussion of the carnivalesque in Rabelais stresses the role the human body plays in the satirist's attempts to level hierarchies by reducing all humans to the same plane. Once naked—once the fact that we all share certain bodily functions is undeniable, humans cannot array themselves by ranks based on birth or wealth or power as readily. Moseley-Braun's foregrounding of black bodies—including her own—served a similar function, for, once the bodily fact of slavery is made visible, politicians cannot escape what bondage meant for her ancestors by using abstractions.

The central argument in the debate was, of course, different, depending on the side you were on. One group wanted to honor the UDC, the symbolic significance of the Confederate flag notwithstanding because, if the flag had that message for some, it did not have that message to many in the South and did not have that message to the UDC. The other group saw the symbolic significance of the flag for African Americans (and others) as the issue and, although willing perhaps to honor the UDC, was not willing to honor the organization with a design patent for that symbol. On both sides, there was a high degree of emotion. Moseley-Braun's physical presence before the debating Senators, however, may be a clue to another argument that those opposed to the patent were offering.

Passive varidirectional double-voiced discourse does not always involve arguments opposed to one another. In this case, the second argument simply goes in another direction. It is a message many in the Senate wanted to send about the Senate: that the Senate does not contain enough diversity to truly understand or represent the people of the United States.

The argument is offered by several in the course of the debate. Referring to Moseley-Braun, Senator Murray, early in the debate, said

> I know her sense of frustration, I recognize her outrage. As a woman, I share some understanding of her situation. But I cannot know her sense of isolation being the only African American in this body. (S 9256)

Later in the debate, Delaware Senator Joseph Biden notes that he "and others have been saying for so long that there is a need for diversity in this body, not need for diversity to have a numerical representation representing the country, but need for diversity" in order to produce "civility and a sense of understanding of the other person's point of view" (S 9260). Senator Boxer made essentially the same point still later in the debate, saying "We are enriched as an institution because the American people made this a more diverse body" by electing Senators such as Moseley-Braun and Campbell (S 9266). Senator John Kerry of Massachusetts put the argument a slightly different way. He noted that "there is a real discomfort as I think about the fact that we are 96 white men and women debating whether or not we ought to be sensitive to the expression of one African American and one Native American. If that," Kerry added, "does not tell us what the problem is, then nothing will" (S 9265). Senator Metzenbaum sounds an "Amen" when he says, "It was long past due that we have a woman of color in the U.S. Senate" (S 9266).

Note how this example of double-voiced discourse and the carnivalesque work together. They both push the point of view of the historically and still disempowered to the fore. They challenge the way the Senate has traditionally done its business, just as the highly personal, highly emotional style of almost all the rhetors does. This challenging of the traditional perhaps brings the debate into something like a circle, for Southern Senators, defending the Confederate flag had insisted that it stood for a Southern tradition that somehow excluded slavery. The rhetoric of those opposed to giving the design patent to the UDC are in essence saying, by their arguments and their ways of arguing, that tradition is often a curtain to hide behind, a curtain that must be ripped aside.

LACK OF FINALIZABILITY

The debate on July 22, 1993, did not begin or end that afternoon. Butler does a good job tracing earlier events of the day—that is, Moseley-Braun's objections to the serious discussion of the *Dred Scott* decision during confirmation hearings for Ruth Bader Ginsburg as Supreme Court Associate Justice—that culminated in this debate. His analysis overcomes the tendency to assign the debate too neat a beginning. Perhaps his analysis should have extended even farther back—beyond Senator Moseley-Braun's arrival in Washington, beyond George Wallace's flying of the Confederate flag in Montgomery to protest federal government action and Robert Kennedy's visit to the Alabama capital city to the Civil War itself and its aftermath in the South. The issue of slavery—and how the Confederate flag symbolized it for many citizens—is not a twentieth-century one.

On the other end of the debate, one needs to read the debate itself for positive and negative hints of how questions of racism will be discussed and understood in the future. Several Senators, most notably Paul Simon of Illinois and Daniel Patrick Moynihan of New York, suggested that the Senate will never be the same—that Moseley-Braun's personal, emotional remarks had jarred the Senate and made it no longer possible to hide behind abstractions such as "patents," devalue matters because they were "history," or fail to see what might be lurking behind matters labeled routine or business-as-usual or honorific or traditional. It was an "epiphany," Moynihan declared (S 9260). Even Senators who in the end still voted against Moseley-Braun voiced their appreciation for her willingness to abandon the "lawyerly" and truly humanize the chamber's discourse.

But then there was Senator Helms' closing remarks, in which he attacked those who "contrived" to bring "the spectre of race" into the debate for "political" and "partisan" reasons (S 9271). In a comment that rushes the Senate back into the abstract, Moseley-Braun's heartfelt comments on racism are labeled "a political ploy to escape responsibility for false pretense that should not have happened in the first place" (S 9271). The conflict between what the many Senators said and what Helms said (or tried to say in the obscure phrase I just quoted) suggested that the nation's confrontation with its racism is not yet over. The debate on July 22 did not reach an end; it was, rather, an important chapter in discourse ultimately not finalizable.

The debate was in the summer of 1993. I am writing this analysis in the summer of 1999—six years later. Just this week, the NAACP has begun "calling for a national boycott of vacation spots in th[e] tourism-dependent state" of South Carolina (Pressley: A3). Why? Because South Carolina is flying the Confederate flag from the top of its statehouse in Columbia. "Just this week, a state Supreme Court justice in Mississippi began hearing a challenge to the Mississippi flag brought by the state NAACP" (Pressley: A3). Why? The Mississippi flag—like that of Georgia—incorporates the Confederate flag within it. As NAACP national director of field operations Nelson Rivers III notes, the flag "is a symbol of oppression and slavery, and it represents probably the biggest symbol of the abuse of African American people." The fact that it is still flown sends the following message: "We've told you for years it offends us, yet you continue to fly it, and that shows you hold us in disregard and much disdain" (Pressley: A3).

The same day this story was featured in the pages of the *Washington Post*, columnist William Raspberry chose to link the flying of the Confederate flag with the city of Richmond's displaying a picture of Robert E. Lee and Supreme Court Chief Justice Rehnquist's leading a 4th Circuit Judicial Conference in the singing of "Dixie." Raspberry is not as upset at the symbolism as Rivers. But the coincidence of these events in the summer of 1999 and the fact that they occurred six years after Carol Moseley-Braun made her stand before the Senate reveals that debates are not finalized by votes or by the sounding of a gavel.

And, as I revise this chapter in the fall of 1999, Helms is threatening to block President Clinton's nomination of Moseley-Braun as United States ambassador to New Zealand. Although "Helms made no mention of Moseley-Braun's successful opposition in 1993 to a Helms proposal that would have renewed the United Daughters of the Confederacy's design patent," the reporter—the *Washington Post*'s Helen Dewar—did. In fact, she cited Helms' comment to another reporter that "At a very minimum she [Moseley-Braun] has got to apologize for the display that she provoked over a little symbol for a wonderful group of little old ladies" or "look for another line of work" (Dewar: A17).

Chapter Four

The Women of the Senate
Remember Tailhook '91

The second debate I have chosen to analyze is the 1994 debate over the retirement rank of Admiral Frank B. Kelso II. This debate was six hours long; and it was dramatic because the seven women in the Senate were united in an attempt to deny the Admiral a four-star retirement. They were so united because he was Chief of Naval Operations during the notorious Tailhook '91 convention in Las Vegas, a convention that featured excessive consumption of alcohol, pornography, sexually-explicit live entertainment, and sexual assault. Furthermore, he was in charge during an investigation the women will repeatedly characterize as "bungled" at best or an attempt to sweep sexual harassment under the carpet at worst.

I have treated this debate at length in an essay in the *Southern Communication Journal*. As I noted in Chapter One, my analysis had two foci: first, I demonstrated that the women successfully used what others have characterized as a "feminine" political style in the debate; second, I demonstrated that the women engaged in double-voiced discourse by offering a text and a less noticeable subtext during the debate. The text spoke directly to the question of two or four stars for Kelso; the subtext raised larger questions about a culture—in and out of the military—that tolerated sexual discrimination, harassment, and assault. This use of double-voiced discourse is, of course, something a Bakhtinian perspective would alert one to. The more concerted application of that paradigm, however, reveals more.

VOICES

A cursory examination of the numerous Senators who spoke reveals that, rather than two sides, there were many voices. If one were to list them, the presence of female voices only on the side opposing the four-star retirement would be immediately noticed, for all seven women in the Senate spoke against four stars for Kelso. But a list would obscure three important dimensions of the orchestration of this example of polyphony: first, that those opposed dominated the beginning of the debate; second, that the debate reached an angry climax when Senator Stevens interrogated Senator Carol Moseley-Braun, and Senators Patty Murray and Barbara Mikulski rose to her defense; third, that after that climax, the debate trailed off into the several minor voices of those who wished to be on the record but not part of the fray. The polyphony thus had a dramatic structure—attack and defense; angry climax; denouement—culminating in an anticlimactic vote (since both floor managers, J. James Exon of Nebraska and Barbara Mikulski of Maryland, knew the likely tally all along). Such a dramatic account is certainly a different rendering of the discussion than one dominated by what the ayes said, what the nays said. It's richer, more human.

A list would at least identify the voices—as individual presentations. And it is important to understand them as such and not to lump them in with the aye side or the nay side, for there were substantive differences among speakers on both sides. For example, on the question of Kelso's presence on the party floor at Tailhook '91 and his having heard and/or seen the disreputable activities, Senators opposed to his retiring with full honors disagreed. Some believed Navy judge William Vest rather than the Department of Defense (D.O.D.) Inspector General (I.G.); others demonstrated their belief in Kelso's integrity and believed him, and the I.G. California Senator Diane Feinstein, for example, found Vest's account more credible:

> I realize that Admiral Kelso's personal involvement and knowledge of the activities which occurred at Tailhook '91 has been in dispute. The DoD Inspector General found "no evidence that Admiral Kelso has specific knowledge of the improper incidents and events that took place" and goes on to say that they "believe" Admiral Kelso did not witness any indecent acts. However, I find a recent ruling by a Navy judge, Captain William Vest, to be quite compelling. (S 4433)

She proceeded to quote at length from Vest's findings. Texas Senator Kay Bailey Hutchinson concluded differently:

During the convention, there has been a dispute about whether Admiral Kelso actually saw any of the debauchery or unseemly behavior. He says he did not. I believe him. (S 4434)

On the question of whether Kelso failed to exercise "due diligence" with regard to Tailhook '91, Senators in favor of four stars disagreed. Some believed he did; others believed his entire record should be considered, not just what they granted was his failure in this case. Georgia Senator Sam Nunn, for example, asked the question "Was it lack of due diligence on his part?" And said "That is what everybody has to ask" (S 4429). Nunn initially said Kelso was so diligent in investigating the events at Tailhook '91 that the Navy "had to be cautioned to apply due process" (S 4429). Minutes later, Nunn admitted, "He could have done better . . . ," but concluded that "there is substantial evidence that he intended the Navy to undertake a proper investigation and that he acted vigorously to combat the problems that were at the root cause of the Tailhook misconduct" (S 4430). Senator Harlan Mathews of Tennessee disagreed:

There is not a Senator among us who condones or excuses the repugnant events of Tailhook '91. Admiral Kelso was present at that event. Testimony by the admiral's superiors before the Armed Services Committee concluded, however, he did not witness any misconduct. Nevertheless, Admiral Kelso is a 38–year veteran of the Navy. He knew the reputation of the Tailhook Symposium, or certainly he should have known. The men involved were active-duty officers, and I suspect that the admiral himself wishes he had taken more direct personal control of its goings-on. But Admiral Kelso has already been judged for his failure to do so in a court of public opinion, whose verdict has been less than generous. . . . Deciding whether Admiral Kelso retires with four stars is a decision that we must base upon his performance throughout an entire career. (S 4444)

Similarly, the individual Senators had different motivations for speaking and for speaking in a certain manner. Senators Alfonse D'Amato of New York and Arlen Specter of Pennsylvania had recently run afoul of women voters during Clarence Thomas' confirmation hearings as Supreme Court Associate Justice: their speaking against Kelso may have been motivated by their need to improve their standing with the female segment of the electorate. Senator Murray, not possessing the legal credentials of many of her colleagues, spoke in a legal manner—perhaps to demonstrate her command of the evidentiary. She began by noting Kelso's "distinguished military career" and defining the precise question before the Senate. Then, she noted how she had carefully reviewed "the documents and history"; then, she proceeded to note what "[t]he evidence suggests" (S 4437). Senators Hutchinson and Nancy Kassebaum of Kansas, the Republican women, spoke fairly briefly—perhaps keeping their political distance from the liberal women they were allied with on this matter. Hutchinson noted her "three areas of concern" and reviewed them methodically, 1–2–3. She saved emotion for a peroration that talked about the future of the Navy (S 4434–35). Kassebaum spoke during the denouement of the debate. She praised Kelso for his "great skill, courage, and ability," but concluded that he "demonstrated a complete failure of leadership in the so-called Tailhook investigation" (S 4456).

Finally, as passages cited later in this chapter will show, some of the women, notably Barbara Boxer of California, Mikulski, and Moseley-Braun, were far more interested than the other women in how Tailhook '91 was part of a patriarchal culture that affected the entire military, commerce, and even the Senate. Others opposed to four stars for Kelso seemed to have their focus on the particular matter at hand, perhaps suggesting their unwillingness to become identified with this more radical stance.

Interestingly, the media played up the fact that the seven women of the U.S. Senate were, with one voice, challenging a special honor for Kelso because of what Tailhook '91 represented. An article by Margaret Carlson in the May 2, 1994 *Time*, for example, treated the seven women as a group, referring to no single female Senator. An article by Linda Palmer in the April 23, 1994 *Congressional Quarterly* noted how "the seven women of the Senate put their colleagues on notice" through "the vehemence of their oratory." In addition, a few of the women even talked about their opposition in these univocal terms. Senator Boxer noted that, "This is the first time that the seven women of the Senate have pulled together across party lines. And I want to say that our unity should be noted" (S 4423). Later, Senator Moseley-Braun reminded her Senate colleagues "that it is no accident that all of the women of this Chamber are of one mind about this issue" (S 4452). However, a more accurate rendition would at least sever the two Republicans from the five (maybe the three) Democrats who were, to varying degrees, offering this larger, more radical argument and trying to offer it, in solidarity, as a gendered group.

INTER-VOICES

This particular debate ran for slightly more than six hours. A detailed analysis of the full polyphony is, therefore, impossible in a single chapter. I intend, as a result, to examine two chunks of discourse, one from each side, just to exemplify the richness of inter-voices that emerge as the speakers speak. Then, I will step back and look at the debate as a whole, for some interesting patterns emerge if one asks if the polyphony varies from speaker to speaker or, more important, from side to side or gender to gender.

Rather than look at Mikulski and Exon, who managed the debate, I want to look at the speakers they seemed to be relying on as chief debaters—California Senator Barbara Boxer for those opposed to Kelso; Georgia Senator Sam Nunn for those in favor.

Boxer, as noted a moment ago, began by making it clear she was speaking for all seven women in the U.S. Senate. She noted how they were speaking as one, across party lines, for the first time ever. Then, after this pluralizing of her voice, she read excerpts from the Department of Defense Inspector General's report on Tailhook '91. She referred to the stories of many victims of sexual harassment and assault at the Las Vegas gathering; she told Victim 28 and Victim 41's stories; and she used Victim 50's own words. The voices of the victims were thus heard.

Boxer then recalled how Secretary of the Navy Garrett had to call in the Inspector General and how the I.G. severely criticized four of the five officers responsible up to that point in the investigation. To give us the I.G.'s voice (not just her summary of it), she entered it into the *Record* as an exhibit. After noting how the I.G. had accused Navy personnel of lying and stonewalling, Boxer gave us Lt. Paula Coughlin's story. Boxer included Coughlin's immediate supervisor's flip response to her complaint of harassment; the Senator quoted the young lieutenant's letter of resignation.

Boxer then referred to hearings conducted by Representative Patricia Schroeder into sexual harassment in the armed forces and how several witnesses spoke at those hearings of their abuse. The story of one in particular, who was locked in a mental ward because she complained, was highlighted.

Boxer then quoted the Inspector General's summary concerning the failure of U.S. Navy leadership in stopping and investigating Tailhook '91. She cited the conflict between the I.G.'s report and the Navy judge's as to where Kelso was and what he heard and saw in Las Vegas. Then she quoted a Vice Admiral, who in 1985 wrote of his concern over Tailhook's annual fete, and the Tailhook Association's President, who wrote in 1991 to squadron leaders about supplying their party suites, responsibility for damage, and the need to combat a late night "gang mentality" among the drunken aviators. She entered his letter into the *Record* and concluded by using the words of the I.G. and the paraphrased conclusion of the Navy judge about Tailhook '91.

Many different kinds of voices find their way into Boxer's discourse. Not as many were in Nunn's.

He began by recalling that Kelso had said he found Tailhook '91 repugnant and by recalling that the Admiral had offered to resign. His civilian supervisors, however, asked Kelso to stay on and fix the problems that Tailhook '91 had revealed. Several voices here.

Having allowed some voices from 1992 to be reheard, Nunn moved to the matter at hand. He noted the Armed Services Committee's endorsement; he referred to his own remarks that were already entered into the *Record*. Nunn then referred repeatedly to what various authorities said: D.O.D. I.G. VanderSchaaf, Secretary of the Navy Dalton, Chairman of the Joint Chiefs of Staff Shalikashvili, and Secretary of State Perry. Nunn then returned to Kelso's voice, paraphrasing the Admiral on a scandalous incident aboard the U.S.S. Iowa and recalling the conversations with the Admiral that convinced him of Kelso's innocence of any wrongdoing. After a hostile question from Senator Mikulski and a friendly one from Virginia Senator John Warner, Nunn returned to the voices of authorities. At one point, he gave voice to "everyone concerned in the Department of Defense."

After another friendly question from Warner, Nunn offered imagined voices: Kelso's, the Senate's in 1992 if the Admiral's retirement rank had been discussed then, and the Senate's now, in 1994, on the issue. Exon then interrupted to cite statistics, Nunn's words four times, President Clinton's once, and the twenty out of twenty-two members of the Armed Services Committee who endorsed four stars for Kelso. Nunn thanked Exon and concluded by calling the women opposing the Admiral "sincere" and saying that all in the Senate condemn Tailhook '91 univocally.

Although not all of the chunks of discourse from the debate are as full of inter-voices as Boxer's and Nunn's, most are. As a result, the critic is left with a rich polyphony and a desperate need for some sort of coding scheme, such as the one I introduced in Chapter Two.

Once the inter-voices in all of the different speakers' remarks are classified, one can see a few—what I'd call—peculiarities. For example, Senator Boxer was the most likely to voice others' stories:

Victim No. 26 was walking through the third floor "gauntlet" when, according to the inspector general, "suddenly men reached out grabbing and groping. . . . She screamed and covered herself with her arms."

Victim No. 41 was also assaulted in the "gauntlet." As she walked into the crowd "men began hooting and hollering at her. A group of men surrounded her and began groping her body. Several men ran their hands up her legs . . . and fondled her. . . . She attempted to defend herself by striking out at them, but as she twisted and turned, another group of men fondled her from behind."

Victim No. 50 was a lieutenant in the Navy. She testified that, as she walked through the third floor hallway a "man . . . moved in immediately behind me with his body pressed against mine. He was bumping me, pushing me forward down the passageway where the group on either side was pinching and pulling at my clothing. The man then put both his hands down the front of my tank top [and grabbed me]. . . . I felt as though the group was trying to rape me." (S 4423–24)

Boxer also voiced her own story:

> Any of us who have had any experience with sexual assault, any of us who have had any experience with sexual harassment, will tell you straight from the heart, you do not forget it. I myself had an experience when I was very young, a senior in college, and I can tell you every single detail of what happened to me. And I was not bleeding and I was not subjected to the same kind of groping and pain that some of these women faced in the gauntlet. (S 4447)

Boxer was also the most likely to recall and repeat what colleagues had said. On the other hand, Senator Murray was the most likely to create the imagined words of others or the Senate. She "quoted" the never-uttered words of the presumed leader: "You are my responsibility. You will be safe"; she imagined the U.S. Senate saying "we do not condone sexual harassment" and then looking the other way in the case of Tailhook '91; she voiced the message men in the armed forces hear as "you can get away with sexual abuse and harassment in the U.S. military"; she had herself said to young women who aspire to a military career "Go ahead, be all that you can be, but don't expect the top person to protect you if you get in a situation that gets out of control—even if she or he is present at the time" (S 4437). Within the last example, Murray either stylized, using the words from the Army's recruiting advertisements—that is, "Be all that you can be," or she used varidirectional passive double-voiced discourse, parodying those encouraging words. And Mikulski and Moseley-Braun were the most likely to evoke back-home or popular culture voices, such as what the lead males might have said and done in movies such as *Top Gun* and *An Officer and a Gentleman* (Mikulski at S 4444) or what kids back in a Chicago neighborhood might say (Moseley-Braun at S 4453). Senators Exon and Ted Stevens of Alaska liked to drop the names of authorities into their discourse, whereas Michigan's Carl Levin, Arizona's John McCain, and Nunn proceeded like lawyers and offered piece after piece of evidence. Nunn's initial presentation, analyzed above, exhibits this pattern. If one were interested in a particular rhetor's style, one might find interesting data in the kind of polyphony he or she creates by including certain kinds of inter-voices.

The more interesting differences, however, separate the pro-Kelso speakers from the anti-Kelso ones. For the sake of clarity, let me proceed one-to-nine through the list of possible inter-voices outlined in Chapter Two. First, the names of authorities were evoked much more by the pro-Kelso Senators. Second, evidence was used equally. Third, stylization rarely appeared. Fourth, references to one's own earlier words were used equally. Fifth, references to colleagues' words were used equally, with Boxer and Warner—on the opposite sides—being the most likely to cite or quote colleagues. Sixth, stories were presented much more by the anti-Kelso speakers, especially by Boxer and Mikulski; seventh, imagined voices (prosopopoeia) were presented much more by the anti-Kelso speakers. Eighth, these anti-Kelso Senators were more likely to speak as "We." Feinstein, for example, says "We, the women of the Senate, have been bringing to public attention the issue of sexual harassment" and "we women are saying . . . it cannot be business as usual in the U.S. military" (S 4432). And, ninth, the anti-Kelso speakers were much more likely to evoke back-home or popular culture voices.

As a result, the polyphony created by the pro-Kelso speakers was very legalistic, with the names and voices of authorities dominant. The polyphony created by the anti-Kelso speakers had these voices *and* the stories of those affected *and* the imagined comments of the principals *and* the imagined messages being delivered by the Senate *and* voices from neighborhoods back home or the movies. Rather than being legalistic, the polyphony was human as well as offering more variety. In addition, the voices often multiplied themselves by being those of "We," not "I." Rather than an adjudication focused on evidentiary matters, this polyphony resembled a raucous town hall meeting or, perhaps, a carnival, filled with the voices of the community's human inhabitants. One should note too that, when the media reported on the debate, they tended to focus on the very voices that distinguished the anti-Kelso speakers from the pro-Kelso speakers: the victims' stories, the "We-ness," and the close-to-home phrases captured the attention, not the evidence-reading.

DOUBLE-VOICING AND CARNIVALESQUE

I am, of course, already suggesting that the anti-Kelso forces were exhibiting what Bakhtin terms the carnivalesque. The solidarity among the once-marginalized women Senators and the women victims of Tailhook '91 brought a noticeable antiestablishment energy to the debate. Although the debate was certainly dealing with serious issues, there was a celebratory feel at times to this energy—for example, when women from the House of Representatives joined their Senate colleagues and Senators Boxer and Mikulski thanked and paid tribute to their House peers:

BOXER: I am very glad to see my colleagues here from the House of Representatives. I had the distinct privilege of serving with many of them and, as a matter of fact, I made a walk over from the House on another matter, that is very close to the one they just made.

MIKULSKI: Senator Boxer, I too wish to acknowledge the presence of our colleagues from the House, many who serve on the Armed Forces Committee, and many who have stood with us on battles for social justice and equal rights and dignity for all. (S 4423)

Additional support for the suggestion that we are dealing with the carnivalesque is found in what I would call the authority structure of the debate. As Senator Exon noted, retirement at the highest rank served had become *pro forma*. As numerous speakers noted, two presidents, two secretaries of Defense, three secretaries of the Navy, and two chairmen of the Joint Chiefs all had endorsed Kelso. Their collective authority was behind the recommended retirement rank, as was the 20–2 authority of the Senate Armed Services Committee, a revered committee. The matter should therefore have been routine, but the women of the Senate (and some men) did not let it be so. And the women were well aware that their collective action challenged—subverted—what is authorized and therefore presumably routine.

Some who speak of Bakhtin's notion of the carnivalesque expect the body, perhaps in its less "proper" manifestations, to be necessarily foregrounded in carnivalesque discourse. As I suggested earlier, Bakhtin seems to construct a continuum of such discourse, the more formal of which would probably not be quite so starkly physical as the less. Nonetheless, the body did indeed play a major role in the discourse of those opposing (particularly the women opposing) a four-star retirement. They did not speak of sexual harassment and assault in abstract terms; rather, they spoke of the particular victims and what specifically had been done to their bodies. The speakers refrained from being explicit:

BOXER: In the interest of decency, Madam President, I will refrain from entering the contents of the Department of Defense inspector general's final report on Tailhook into the Record. (S 4423)

FEINSTEIN: There were incidents that took place which, frankly, I do not want to mention on the Senate floor. I do not believe it is appropriate. (S 4432)

MIKULSKI: It is very hard to debate this on the Senate floor. The reason it is hard is that when one reads what happened in Tailhook, and when one hears about the chants that Admiral Kelso allegedly heard and turned his back on, it is so vulgar I cannot bring myself to even read from the report on the Senate floor. I will not do that to the Senate. But let me say to the American people watching on C-SPAN, because that is where it is [*sic*], it is pretty bad. In fact, it is so bad that we, the women of the Senate, do not wish to use the type of language that is described. (S 4444)

Nonetheless, the women left no doubt as to the bodily reality of what occurred at Tailhook '91. They furthermore made it clear that they did not want this bodily reality lost in the abstractions and generalizations characteristic of authorized U.S. Senate discourse. They wanted the bodily reality—even the vulgarity—to be known, even if not actually heard: rhetorically shrewd "un-voiced discourse" (if I can coin a term).

As I suggested earlier, one type of voicing, what Bakhtin terms "varidirectional passive double-voiced" discourse, is quite consonant with the carnivalesque. In this debate, we find at least two examples of such voicing. On a small scale, some of the women used military language parodically. Thereby, the authority such language usually entails is opposed by the attitude toward it implicit in the parody. Mikulski, for example, responded to attacks on herself and her female colleagues by noting that, "It [was] the U.S. Navy and the men who served under Kelso that torpedoed the career of Frank Kelso. . . ." (S 4423); she also, later in the debate, noted that

Here we have a whole U.S. Navy, it equipped itself with night optics, but it has myopia when it goes to investigate this matter. Well, put your goggles on, guys. It is time to look and see what is going on. (S 4445)

On a larger scale, the women voiced a set of arguments against Kelso's four-star promotion while, simultaneously, voicing a set of arguments about the culture—in and out of the military—that tolerates events such as Tailhook '91. These somewhat hidden arguments surfaced later in the debate. Mikulski referred to "old habits, old attitudes, and a very old and dying culture" (S 4448); Moseley-Braun said, "Tailhook represents the most reprehensible, the worst aspect of women in the workplace, and that is sexual harassment, sexual abuse, and sexual assault" (S 4452–53). She was no longer speaking about just the military. Mikulski finally made the subtext more explicit as the debate climaxed:

> Mr. President, . . . we must change the culture, and this very debate is about changing the culture. We hope we win this. But whether we win the vote or not, we feel that we have won a victory here today because we have raised this issue to show that from now on when we look at what is going to happen in promotions and in retirements and in rewards, the issues will be raised, and they will be raised not only about the United States military, they will be raised about the FBI, they will be raised about the Bureau of Alcohol and Firearms, they will be raised about Social Security, they will be raised about the gender discrimination going on at the National Institutes of Health. They will be raised. (S 4453)

This subtext, as I suggested in the *Southern Journal of Communication* essay, parodied the more obvious text, suggesting that the text missed the more important broad issues that the debate was truly about (62). In addition, this parodic relationship between subtext and text suggested that the men arguing for the higher honor for Kelso were very much imprisoned within the indicted culture. Either that or they enjoyed such a position of power within that culture that they could tolerate and ignore the message in the subtext.

An important question needs, therefore, to be addressed: is the women's carnivalesque subversion an authorized and thereby illusory subversion? This question is rooted in Bakhtin's writings, for he suggests that the carnivalesque can fade into "reduced laughter" as the energy, no matter how subversive it is thought to be, becomes encapsulated within established forms (Morson and Emerson: 463–65). This reduction is, of course, the danger as a subversive rhetor moves along the carnivalesque continuum from folk carnival to Rabelais to novel to something formal (such as a Senate debate).

No definitive answer to the question is possible. However, there are several clues in the six-hour debate that the authority structure being challenged did not understand what was happening. The carnivalesque has, as one might expect, an emotional quality to it that contrasts sharply with the legalistic exposition offered by pro-Kelso speakers. These pro-Kelso speakers sensed the power within emotion, but they did not understand how to control it. Some, for example Senators Harlan Mathews of Tennessee and Daniel Coats of Indiana, said they respected it but did not believe policy should be based on it. Mathews, as noted earlier, referred to the events of Tailhook '91 as "repugnant," cited testimony that absolves Kelso of personal involvement, noted that Kelso could have done better, and then asked that the decision on four stars be "base[d] upon his performance throughout an entire career" (S 4444). Coats opened his remarks by addressing Tailhook '91. He said, "Tailhook was an ugly incident. I am pleased to be able to use the past tense, because it is an incident that will not be repeated." He then observed that, "No one on this Senate floor condones what happened at Tailhook." Having offered a pro forma nod at Tailhook's abuses, he then shifted the question:

> The question before us, I believe, is whether we look at what has transpired in the Navy since the occurrence of this particular incident and others, or whether we make a final point by demoting a man who has given 38 years of service in the service of his country and reached the pinnacle of success in the branch of service that he has served in. (S 4443)

Coats' answer was obvious in his language. And, tellingly, he managed to move from the ugliness of Tailhook '91 to Kelso's achieving "the pinnacle of success" in just four sentences. He, in essence, pushed the issue of sexual harassment—and emotional responses to it—aside, as had Mathews.

Others tried to imitate the rhetorical strategy of making emotional appeals but failed. Senator Warner responded to the emotion-laden stories about the victims of Tailhook '91 by voicing the story of Admiral Kelso's wife, who will be victimized if the Senate reduces her husband's pension:

> But I hope that those who are debating here today would broaden the word punishment to include Admiral Kelso's partner for 38 years in the U.S. Navy, his wife and his family. . . . For 38 years, Mrs. Kelso has packed and unpacked and traveled throughout the world, as have other Navy wives, other Army wives, other Air Force wives, other Marine

Corps wives. Military service is a partnership. It is a family. Part of that
punishment will be monetary. . . . Madam President, I ask the chairman,
is that fair to the Navy family? Is that fair to a wife? (S 4429)

Senator Stevens responded by briefly voicing the story of the Admiral's
daughters. Stevens' story was too brief and too vague to have any effect;
Warner's was aptly characterized by Senator Boxer as "a disconnect," who
added sarcastically, "I do not know what the point was in bringing her name
into this. Was it to give a message to the women of the Senate that we are
hurting another woman; namely, Mrs. Kelso" (S 4447). Minnesota Senator
David Durenberger, speaking for Kelso, even offered the story of a woman
victimized by sexual harassment long after Tailhook '91 had alerted the
Navy to its problem. Her voice was really one for those opposing the Admiral's cause. These Senators could not use the strategy the women used so
well; therefore, it is difficult to conceive of the men as being in ultimate control of the rhetorical situation and allowing the carnivalesque energy.

In addition, those speaking from the authorized position got genuinely
angry at those opposing Kelso's four-star retirement. Several men expressed their anger, denouncing a "no" vote in strong terms. The best example of anger, however, was clearly that of Senator Stevens. Senator Boxer
described him as angry; he admitted he was (S 4450). Then, he proceeded to
lash out at her and, later, to harass and insult Senator Moseley-Braun. She
took a few minutes "so that I can calm down" (S 4453), while Senators
Murray and Mikulski defended her. Mikulski said:

Mr. President, during this entire debate, the women of the Senate and
the men who support us in this cause have attempted to conduct this
debate with civility and courtesy. The distinguished Senator from Illinois knows full well that the President of the United States made this
request. We know full well it was the Secretary of Defense, Secretary
of Navy, and Joint Chiefs. We know that. That does not make a difference. The fact is—and the Senator from Illinois knows that full
well—we, the women of the Senate, are not stupid. We know the rules.
(S 4453)

Encouraged by Mikulski's response to Stevens' badgering questions,
Moseley-Braun then accused Stevens of violating the rules of the Senate by
his discourteous, chauvinistic remarks. Anger had, as a viewing of the exchange would make clear, caused Senator Stevens to lose control (Sheckels:
60–61, 65–66). Such a loss is not characteristic of a representative of an au-

thority structure who is permitting the carnivalesque. My conclusion, therefore, is that the carnivalesque polyphony demonstrated here was genuinely subversive.

LACK OF FINALIZABILITY

When one examines the media coverage of this debate, one might think the forces challenging the four-star retirement rank had won, for the women—their solidarity and the message in the subtext—drew the media's attention. Palmer in *Congressional Quarterly* said the women "put their colleagues on notice"; Carlson in *Time* said the women "forced" "the militarists" "to regroup" and "forced a daylong debate." Perhaps the women represented the better story, but, perhaps, the media sensed something happening that made the vote that supposedly finalized the matter an illusory ending. The women seemed to sense as much: toward the debate's end, they talked in terms of what behaviors would no longer go unquestioned and what behaviors would no longer be allowed *because* of this debate. They pointed beyond the vote to both the changes they envisioned and the rhetorical action they pledged. As Mikulski exclaimed, the interconnected issues of sexual discrimination, harassment, and assault "will be raised," "not only about the United States military" but about a range of government agencies and government programs (S 4453).

The vote did not end the full communication event, which, as Mikulski suggested, will be ongoing. What the women were doing was more profound than setting the agenda for future sessions or situating themselves for future elections. Rather, in recognition of the debate's lack of finalizability, they were announcing the continuation of the dialogue and implicitly suggesting that, as the polyphony proceeded, the subversion that characterized this particular debate might eventually be less necessary if and when power imbalances diminished. In the minds of the women, the debate had only begun. And their "saying" this was not "mere rhetoric" but a Bakhtinian reality.

The debate also did not begin with President Clinton's recommendation that Kelso retire with four stars. Mikulski, in her very first speech, foregrounds the question of Kelso:

This is not only an issue about women. Men must also speak up. I said this at the conclusion of the Anita Hill hearings. After we had gone through the intense hearings and debate on Anita Hill, I said this:

I call upon the men of the United States of America now to speak out on the issue of sexual harassment. This is not a women's issue. It is an issue that profoundly affects men and women, and I call upon the men to claim the power that they have in order to speak out and speak up, to be able to speak up about this issue. I call upon the men to speak out in the workplace, to speak out in the newspapers, to speak out in talk shows, to speak out in the gym the way they have spoken to me. And I say if you speak out and you speak up, you may prevent what has happened to your wife or to your daughter, but you will help others elsewhere.

I also said this to the women watching during that time. I said to them: Do not lose heart, but we will lose ground. And we have lost ground. Otherwise, we would not be debating this today. I said to the women: I know how you feel the sting of this, how you feel betrayed and bullied whenever you have been a victim of much sexual harassment. Speak up to a friend. And if you are ever harassed, take good notes. When you speak up, make sure you are not alone, because there will be few there to protect you. (S 4423)

The accusations of sexual harassment that Anita Hill voiced against Clarence Thomas, nominee to the Supreme Court, went unbelieved in 1991—at least by the men who heard the testimony. Anita Hill's accusations, however, quickly became everywoman's. That they were not heard, Mikulski suggested, set the stage for the future harassment, including that as flagrant and as violent as that at Tailhook '91.

"Anita Hill" functioned in the debate over Kelso's retirement rank as a reminder. It reminded those who were attentive that the debate had begun long before the six-hour debate over Kelso's four stars. Mikulski talked about Hill's testimony later in the debate (S 4448), mentioning how Americans were glued to their television sets, watching the proceedings. Other women made it very clear that 1991—the year of both Hill's testimony and the notorious Tailhook Symposium—is not 1994. Things have changed. As Boxer notes, "Senator Nunn asked a very important question, and I admit, it made me think: What would we have done if this matter had come to us in 1992 on the floor of the U.S. Senate." Nunn had argued that the approval of four stars would have been virtually automatic. Boxer says:

It is important to recall that in 1992, Senator Carol Moseley-Braun was not in the U.S. Senate. She came here in 1993 with me, Senator Murray, and Senator Feinstein, and we joined Senator Mikulski. Senator Hutchinson was not here, either. So I do not know what would have happened in 1992. Knowing my colleague, Senator Mikulski,

who knows? She may have taken this battle on and stood on her feet
hour after hour, hopefully with Senator Kassebaum. (S 4447)

Boxer's point was that there were in 1994 seven women, not two in the Senate. As Mikulski suggested elsewhere in the debate, the viewing of "Anita
Hill undergo[ing] one of the most serious, grueling, humiliating experi-
ences that anyone has ever endured before the U.S. Senate" (S 4448) played
a role in increasing the number of women in that body.

The debate on April 19, 1994, then, did not begin when Senator Mitchell
asked that the Senate proceed to executive session to consider item number
828. Mikulski suggested that it had begun earlier, when the matter of sexual
harassment was first brought to light—when what had been a fact of life for
women in various environments had first been named. The debate also did
not end on April 19. On the positive side, the larger issues raised in the debate's subtext have been frequently raised since then. On the negative, the
U.S. Navy announced on January 20, 1999 that "it is restoring relations with
the Tailhook Association." The *Washington Post* quoted Navy Secretary
Richard Danzig as saying, "We've concluded that the time is right to restore
ties" ("Navy to Restore": A7). The "we" includes the top officers of both the
Navy and the Marine Corps. Let's hope "the time is right" not because nine
years have passed and people have forgotten.

Chapter Five

Bob Smith and Barbara Boxer Duel

The third debate considered in this study was held over several days in December 1995 (S 17881–S 18187). It dealt with a bill that would ban a medical procedure some termed "partial-birth abortion."

VOICES

The debate over Kelso's retirement rank was an emotional six-and-a-half hours. The debate over "partial-birth abortion" was emotional, but it was not as sustained. Just as long, it took place in four installments. If one were to list who spoke, one would rather quickly see that this debate was less polyphonous than many, as two speakers, Republican Robert Smith of New Hampshire (for the ban) and Democrat Barbara Boxer of California (against), dominated, turning the discussion at times into more a duel than a debate.

Each had allies. However, the way the allies entered the debate differed. Smith's allies spoke early; Boxer's came in more toward the end. Both Smith and Boxer were emotionally engaged in the debate, so much so that both suffered from incoherence at times. Curiously, as fatigue and emotion took their toll on Smith, his colleagues backed off; but, as fatique and emotion took their toll on Boxer, her colleagues came to her assistance. There is perhaps a gender-based gloss one might offer to this difference, for research has shown that men are less comfortable dealing with emotional displays than women (Lewis and McCarthy, Saurer and Eisler, Tannen). Smith's allies, all male, may have quite simply not known how to intervene in his aid.

Also, research has shown that women are more likely to be affiliative (Johnson, Wood and Inman). Boxer's allies, largely female, may have aided her out of a desire to be affiliative, and the emotionally-charged atmosphere did not act as a deterrent for them.

The drama of this debate was then different from that of either of the previous examples. There was a similar tendency to let the major players debate before streams of others put in their brief words, pro or con. That structure may well be somewhat generic. However, there was no sense of climax. Rather, there was a sense of monotony—and exhaustion—as Smith and Boxer kept making the same arguments repeatedly and only occasionally responded to each other.

Several amendments gave the debate a structure of a sort. In response to the concern on both sides of the question that the bill's exception for the life of the mother was not sufficiently strong, Bob Dole of Kansas offered an amendment. That amendment was countered by one by Boxer (and others). Thus, for a long period of time, speakers were addressing these competing amendments as well as the bill itself. Once Dole's amendment was accepted and Boxer's rejected, the Senate dealt quickly with an amendment offered by Hank Brown of Colorado to prevent "dead-beat dads" from bringing legal action against physicians and others under the aegis of the bill, and then the Senate dealt not as quickly with an amendment offered by David Pryor of Arkansas that concerned the extraneous issue of international trade in pharmaceuticals. Then, Diane Feinstein of California offered, in the guise of an amendment, a substitute motion designed to replace the proposed ban with a statement reaffirming the principles enunciated in *Roe v. Wade*. Once that substitute was defeated, the bill itself was approved. Of course, President Clinton vetoed the bill, so its approval was something of a moot point.

Despite the semblance of a structure these amendments provided, the debate featured a great deal of repetition. Boxer—and allies—argued that third-term abortions were medically necessary, that the proposed bill was, in Feinstein's words, "so vague that I believe it will affect more than any one single procedure" (S 18002) and thus, in Washington Senator Patty Murray's words, "instill fear and confusion in the doctors who perform abortions . . . and deter them from performing a procedure that may help save a woman whose life is in danger" (S 18190). They argued that the Senate should not practice medicine and, rather, should leave the selection of appropriate procedures up to the woman and her physician. Smith—and allies—argued that the bill banned one and only one horrific procedure. They stressed its horror.

INTER-VOICES

Since Smith and Boxer so dominated the debate, the inter-voices they used are the most noteworthy ones. Interestingly—especially in light of the analysis of the preceding debate along gender lines—Smith cited authorities, quoted authorities, cited himself, and referred to colleagues much more than Boxer; Boxer told the stories of those affected by the matter under discussion. For example, she told—at great length—the story of Colleen Costello:

I am a registered Republican and very conservative. I do not believe in abortion. Because of my deeply held Christian beliefs, I knew that I would never have an abortion. Then on March 24th of this year when I was 7 months pregnant, I was having premature contractions and my husband and I rushed to the hospital.

During an ultrasound, the physician became very silent. Soon, more physicians came in. I knew in my heart that there was something terribly wrong. I went into the bathroom and I sobbed. I begged God to let my baby be okay. I prayed like I have never prayed before in my life. . . .

My doctor arrived at 2:00 in the morning. He held my hand and informed me that they did not expect our baby to live. She was unable to absorb any amniotic fluid and it was puddling into my uterus. This was causing my contractions. This poor precious child had a lethal neurological disorder and had been unable to move for almost 2 months. The movements I had been feeling over the past months had been nothing more than bubbles and fluid.

Her chest cavity had been unable to rise and fall to stretch her lungs to prepare them for air. Therefore, they were left severely underdeveloped, almost to the point of not existing. Her vital organs were atrophying. Our darling little girl was dying.

A perinatalist recommended terminating the pregnancy. For my husband and me, this was not an option. . . . At this time, we chose our daughter's name. We named her Katherine Grace. . . .

I considered a Cesarean section, but experts at Cedar-Sinai Hospital were adamant that the risks to my health and possibly my life were too great. There was no reason to risk leaving my children motherless if there was no hope of saving Katherine. The doctors all agreed that our only option was the intact D & E procedure. . . .

When I was put under anesthesia, Katherine's heart stopped. She was able to pass away peacefully inside my womb, which was the most comfortable place for her to be. . . .

When I awoke a few hours later, she was brought into us. She was beautiful. She was not missing any part of her brain. She had not been stabbed in the head with scissors. She looked peaceful. . . .

Due to the safety of this procedure, I am again pregnant now. Fortunately, most of you will never have to walk through the valley we have walked. It deeply saddens me that you are making a decision having never walked in our shoes. . . .

What happened to our family is heartbreaking and it is private, but we have chosen to share our story with you because we hope it will help you act with wisdom and compassion. I hope you can put aside your political differences, your positions on abortion, and your party affiliations and just try to remember us. We are the ones who know. We are the families that ache to hold our babies, to love them, to nurture them. We are the families who will forever have a hole in our hearts. We are the families that had to choose how our babies would die. Each one of you should be grateful that you and your families have not had to face such a choice. I pray that no one you love ever does.

Please put a stop to this terrible bill. Families like mine are counting on you. (S 17888)

Boxer's stories were supplemented by those told by others. For example, Illinois Senator Paul Simon introduced the lengthy story of Viki Wilson into the debate, a Catholic woman who believed it was her mission to oppose the proposed law:

I've often wondered why this had happened to us, what we had done to deserve such pain. I am a practicing Catholic. I couldn't help believing that God had to have some reason for giving us such a burden. Then I found out about this legislation, and I knew then and there that Abigail's life had a special meaning. God knew I would be strong enough to come here and tell you our story, to try to stop this legislation from passing and causing incredible devastation for other families like ours. (S 17890)

Once these stories are told, they are repeated by Boxer as well as others opposed to the proposed ban. The effect is somewhat choral. The proponents, however, did have their story as well. They parried Boxer's thrusts with the story of Brenda Pratt:

I am Brenda Pratt, a registered nurse with 13 years of experience. One day in September, 1993, my nursing agency assigned me to work at a Dayton, Ohio, abortion clinic. I had often expressed pro-choice views to my two teenage daughters, so I thought this assignment would be no problem for me. But I was wrong. I stood at a doctor's side as he performed the partial-birth abortion procedure, and what I saw is branded forever on my mind. The mother was 8 months pregnant. The baby's heartbeat was visible, clearly, on the ultrasound. The doctor went in with forceps and grabbed the baby's legs and pulled them down through the birth canal. Then he delivered the baby's body and the arms, everything but the head. The doctor kept the baby's head just inside the uterus. The baby's little fingers were clasping and unclasping and his feet were swinging.

Then the doctor stuck the scissors through the back of his head, and the baby's arms jerked out in a flinched, startled reaction, like a baby when he thinks he might fall. The doctor opened up the scissors, stuck a high-powered suction tube into the opening, and sucked the baby's brains out. Now, the baby was completely limp. (S 17886)

Despite this narrative moment, Boxer, not Smith, was clearly the storyteller in the debate. She also used prosopopoeia slightly more than Smith. But, before we jump to a simplistic gender-based conclusion, we should note that the second biggest storyteller was Edward Kennedy of Massachusetts and that Feinstein was just as likely to quote authorities and refer to colleagues as Smith. But, unlike the men, she rarely simply cited authorities. However, Illinois' Carol Moseley-Braun did tend to just name names. What the analysis then seems to show is highly individualized styles of using inter-voices with some tendency for the males and females to conform partially to gender norms.

Again, as I suggested earlier, a line of research that might well be interesting would be to look at a given Senator's "style" of using inter-voices. Just looking at these first three debates, one can see characteristic styles for Boxer, Feinstein, Smith, Moseley-Braun, and others. Boxer shares the stories of constituents and refers to the remarks of colleagues, building a community on her side of the issue. Feinstein quotes authorities, carefully substantiating each argument as she proceeds. She sounds like a prosecuting attorney. Smith proceeds in a similar manner, except he—unlike Feinstein—exhibits a tendency to refer to his own previous voicings often. Moseley-Braun shoots from the proverbial hip, making it clear to colleagues how she sees matters without being burdened by many citations or quotations. She tosses in a few names but does not allow references to slow her down. With a more exhaustive and more systematic research protocol, one might derive stylistic portraits of key legislators as rich as those Hart has derived for presidents and offered in *Verbal Style and the Presidency* (1984).

DOUBLE-VOICING AND CARNIVALESQUE

If one were to use a flowchart to record this debate and the one discussed in the previous chapter, one would discover that their structures are quite different. As I argued in an essay in the *Southern Communication Journal,* in the debate over Kelso's retirement rank several arguments developed over the course of the speeches. In the debate over the "partial-birth abortion" ban, there was very little development. Smith repeatedly expressed his horror at the procedure; Boxer repeatedly told the story of women whose lives were saved; Smith, joined by Michael DeWine of Ohio, pointed out that these women did not undergo the procedure the bill would outlaw:

DEWINE: [T]he two witnesses who testified in front of our committee . . . gave some very heart-wrenching testimony. No one could have sat through that hearing without being moved, touched. . . . I think, though, that what we need to remember is that neither of these two tragic situations would have been affected by the bill we are debating. . . . We will continue to hear, I am sure, on this floor the argument made that we should look at these two heart-wrenching situations. I simply remind my colleagues, whether in the Chamber or back in their office listening to this debate, that we all agree these are just heart-wrenching situations. But we also should understand, and I ask my colleagues to keep in mind, that these two situations are simply not covered by this bill, and so it is really a bogus argument. (S 17896)

SMITH: [T]he next two witnesses that the supporters of partial-birth abortion presented—and this is the interesting part—were two women who had late-term abortions. . . . The stories they told before the committee were very compelling and very emotional, and I respect that. I understand it. But they were not partial-birth abortions. (S 17901)

In response, Boxer just repeated their stories. Smith, expressing his horror still more times, grew increasingly impatient at Boxer's lack of responsiveness to his charge of the stories' irrelevance:

Again, these things never cease to amaze me. Also, Senator Boxer of California, a few moments ago again referred to the case of Colleen Costello, who spoke very passionately—and it was a compelling story—before the committee of her terrible tragedy of losing a child. And, again, Mr. President, let me repeat that Miss Costello's abortion was not a partial-birth abortion. So that is not what we are talking about here today. (S 18006)

This is really an interesting debate, and I said last night, Viki Wilson's story is truly a tragedy and my heart goes out to Viki Wilson. . . . My bill, the bill that is on the floor before us, or the amendments, would not have precluded Viki Wilson from that procedure. (S 18083)

DeWine jumped in—equally frustrated, but less angry:

Let me repeat for my friends on the floor and my friends who may be watching this on TV that Viki Wilson did not have this procedure. I do not know how many times we have to say it. That is what the facts are. None of the three women did. It is simply not true. (S 18085)

Then, Smith protested some more:

There is only one problem, and I have said it, Senator DeWine has said it and others have said it: These women did not have partial-birth abortions. I will repeat, these women did not have partial-birth abortions. Collen Costello and Viki Wilson did not have partial-birth abortions. Senator Boxer knows that. . . . This is the floor of the U.S. Senate. We have an obligation to tell the truth. That is not the truth, what Senator Boxer is saying. (S 18195)

Finally, Boxer began repeating arguments introduced into the debate by Feinstein, Murray, and others that the bill was vague. She argued that that vagueness will deter women and doctors from undergoing or undertaking any procedure similar to the banned one, thereby significantly reducing a woman's right to choose. Whether the bill is vague or not is not for us to decide. What we need to consider is why Boxer proceeded as she did. Was she a poor debater, one who repeats and refuses to clash? Was she fraying under the emotional weight of what she characterized as "the most unpleasant week that I can remember here in a long time for me personally" (S 18086)? Or was the delaying, which facilitated the telling and retelling of women's stories, and the late-in-the-debate stress on the bill's supposedly unintended chilling effect, strategic?

If Boxer's rhetoric was strategic, there was a kind of varidirectional passive double-voiced discourse operating here. On the surface, there was a debate, but the surface matters little. Just beneath the surface were the stories about real women. They were presented as hostile voices, voices crying "No" to the proposed ban. Furthermore, they were kept in the debate for, perhaps, longer than relevant, so that the hostile "No" voice was heard often. Although these voices were presented as saying "No" to the ban, they were actually saying "No" to any restrictions on the options a woman may choose among, for, given how the pro-choice women saw the "pro-life" agenda, they believed that one restriction would lead to another and then another. Boxer made this point briefly, early in the debate when she said:

> Yes, there are those who want to make [abortion] a crime. They want to put the women in jail. We will get to that another day, I assure you, if they win this one, that is coming down the road. (S 17887)

She elaborated on it somewhat later:

> Well, I think I know what the real agenda is. I do not think it is a surprise. It is not going to shatter anybody's mind when I say this. I think there is a group of Senators who want to make abortion illegal in this country. They ran on that platform. They are committed to doing it. They feel a woman should not have the right to choose.
>
> If it was up to them, they would criminalize this procedure. They would put the woman in jail. They would put the doctor in jail. They do not have the votes, folks. They do not have the votes to outlaw abortion. They wish they did. . . . So these Senators are trying to outlaw abortion not directly but indirectly. (S 17897)

Feinstein stated this larger question in restrained terms:

> [T]his bill is very carefully crafted to provide a direct challenge to *Roe versus Wade*. . . . I believe that the language in this bill, Mr. President, is vague for very deliberate reasons, because by making it vague every doctor that performs even a second-trimester abortion could face the possibility of prosecution in that he or she could be hauled before a court and have to defend their abortion. So this bill in effect could affect all abortions. (S 18002)

Boxer then named some of the past actions and some of the prospective actions that comprise "the plan of the far right" (S 17897) on abortion.

Senator Moseley-Braun used more effusive language. Furthermore, she sketched out the immediate historical context in which this particular bill, she argued, should be seen:

> Madam President, I continue to be astounded when I consider the extent to which a woman's constitutional right to choice has been taken away in this, the 104th Congress.
>
> First came the Hyde amendment limiting a poor woman's reproductive choice because Government contributed to the payment of her health care. Then came the battle of parental notification, limiting very young women in their reproductive choices because of their age—not their condition. Then came the battle over military hospitals, limiting military women in their reproductive choices because they or their spouse chose to serve their country. Then came the battle over Federal health insurance, limiting Federal employees and their reproductive choices because they work for the Government.
>
> [T]he concept of reproductive freedom is under assault. Choice is a matter of freedom. Choice is a fundamental issue of the relationship of female citizens to their Government. Choice is a barometer of equality and a measure of fairness. Choice is central to our liberty.
>
> . . . Today, the assault on reproductive choice has taken on a new ferocity. (S 18080)

After this review of the battle, she offered a revision of Martin Niemoller's poem about the holocaust, titling her rewrite "The Assault on Reproductive Rights":

> First they came for poor women and I did not speak out—because I was not a poor woman.
> Then they came for the teenagers and I did not speak out—because I was no longer a teenager.
> Then they came for women in the military and I did not speak out—because I was not in the military.
> Then they came for women in the Federal Government and I did not speak out—because I did not work for the Government.
> Then they came for the doctors and I did not speak out—because I was not a doctor.
> Then they came for me—and there was no one left to speak out for me. (S 18081)

After melodramatically linking the assault on reproductive rights to the Nazi extermination of Jews, Moseley-Braun declared the fight she and others are waging to be "a quintessential fight for freedom" (S 18081). A bit later, Maryland's Barbara Mikulski, in a more restrained manner, characterized the bill as "a direct assault on *Roe versus Wade*," as "part of a concerted effort to ban all abortions" (S 18189).

Late in the debate, others repeated the argument that those who were supporting the ban have a larger argument in view. And they—most notably Kennedy, Mikulski, and Russell Feingold of Wisconsin—began to offer proof of a sort:

KENNEDY: This political excursion into the practice of medicine is plainly inappropriate. So why is it before the Senate? The answer is simple. The right-to-life movement has brought this bill to Congress in the hope that its passage will advance their goal of discrediting *Roe versus Wade* and eventually outlawing all abortions. The bill's supporters in the House boasted of such a strategy. At least one witness at the committee hearing spoke frankly of the broader agenda. (S 18184)

MIKULSKI: Proponents of this bill have made clear they want to ban all abortions, one procedure at a time, one woman at a time. (S 18190)

FEINGOLD: [T]here is little doubt that the purpose behind this legislation is to begin the process of curtailing and ultimately denying all access to legal abortion. When pressed, many of the proponents of H.R. 1833 will admit the truth of this assertion. One of the major House proponents, Congressman Chris Smith (R. N.J.), stated in a November 9, 1995 *USA Today* article, "We will begin to focus on the methods [of abortion] and declare them to be illegal." (S 18193)

The voices were really making an argument larger than the case offered by Smith, Utah's Orrin Hatch, DeWine, and others warranted. Smith and his allies wanted to talk about partial-birth abortion; the voices were refusing to focus on the small issue at hand. We have, then, much as in the previous example, a subtext that was being eventually pushed into the open as the text—the narrower debate—was being argued in frustrating circles.

In the debate over Kelso's retirement rank, the hostile subtext surfaced when Senator Stevens attacked Senator Moseley-Braun. In the debate over "partial-birth abortion," nothing quite so dramatic brought the subtext to the surface. It gradually emerged. However, its emergence did coincide with that point in the drama when the other women of the Senate (and a few men, such as Kennedy) began coming to Boxer's aid. It also coincided with the point in the drama when the ban's opponents started speaking in terms of "We."

This subtext then functions much as the subtext in the Kelso debate. It is similarly varidirectional passive double-voiced discourse; it takes the debate in a direction other than the one the immediate matter seems to warrant; furthermore, it is parodic, in a broad sense of that word, insofar as it suggests how the immediate task orientation of much authorized discourse obscures larger issues—or maybe is used to obscure larger issues. More narrowly parodic is something you have to see the debate to appreciate. Those supporting the ban, most notably Smith, used anatomical charts to illustrate the medical procedure they sought to ban:

As I remind my colleagues today what a partial-birth abortion is, I am going to again use a series of illustrations that depict the partial-birth abortion procedure. I have done this before on the floor. I have been criticized for it. The press has not gotten it right. Some of them have not gotten it right. I was accused of showing photographs of aborted babies. I was accused of displaying a rubber fetus, whatever that is, all kinds of distortions of the record.

But what I have here are simple medical diagrams. That is all they are. They simply say what the procedure is and simply show it in pictures. I am going to show it again briefly here to show what we mean by partial-birth abortion because I think we should understand what it is.

As I do, keep in mind that these illustrations have appeared in the American Medical Association's official newspaper, the *AMA News*. These are not my drawings. They are not drawn by the pro-life movement. (S 17885)

Smith's protests notwithstanding, in line with the "pro-life" position, the charts clearly depicted a baby; rather curiously, the charts did not show the face of the mother. Rather, she was a decapitated, almost disemboweled, rather dehumanized "thing." Boxer countered the charts by, throughout the entire debate, putting up pictures of the women whose stories she told. She drew explicit attention to these pictures on many occasions, as the following collage of quotations suggests:

I am going to show you a photograph of this woman and her family. . . . I want you to keep that face in mind and the faces of this family in mind. (S 17888)

So what I am going to do during this debate is concentrate on putting a mother's face on the screen and putting her family's face on the screen, and tell her story because it has been left out of this debate. (S 17888)

So I am going to put the face of the mother on this debate. (S 17889)

The reason I am keeping this family portrait up here is because I want to keep this family's face right up here. Because with all the talk about medicine and all the charts of drawings of medical procedures, as if we were a medical school here, this has been forgotten. (S 17897)

We want to put a woman's face on it. We see these drawings. Time after time, day after day—where is the face of the mother? Where is the face of her husband? Where is the face of her children? (S 17898)

What I did last night, and what I intend to do throughout the course of this debate—I will not go on at length tonight—is to try and put the woman's face on this issue. We see many times my colleague from New Hampshire bring out the diagram, and it shows the lower part of a woman's body. It is almost as if a woman's body is a vessel. It does not show the woman's face. It does not show her anguish when she learns that her baby is in serious trouble and could even die if she went forward with birth. So it is my intention to put that face on. (S 18005)

As we get back to this bill, and I understand we will be back to it tomorrow evening about 5, I am going to bring out those photos of those women who have shared their stories with the Senate and want to share it with the American people and let us get this issue out there. (S 18005)

Viki Wilson has two other children. This is Viki Wilson. She is 39. Her husband is Bill. . . . These are their two children. John is 10 and Katie is 8. . . . I want to talk about her story. . . . Mr. President, it is a story that will move you. It is a story that was told to the Judiciary Committee, and while you are going to see posters of part of a woman's body drawn like a cartoon, as if a woman is simply a vessel, we are putting a face on this. (S 18083)

[W]e have just heard a very loud and angry voice [Smith's]. I do not know who that anger is aimed at. . . . I want to say that the anger that you just saw displayed on this floor, in reality, is aimed at families like this in the picture. (S 18084)

I wish to put a face to the women in this debate, so night after night as Senator Smith and I have debated this issue, I have shown the faces of different families who have had to face this tragedy who are never shown on the posters that the other side has used during this debate. (S 18186)

I will hold up picture after picture of people who know that this bill applies to the procedures they had. (S 18196)

We have seen these families night after night. We have seen charts of part of a woman's body, as if she had no face. (S 18198)

Her foregrounding the woman with these periodic statements is, of course, in line with her position which privileges the woman's right to choose. Rhetorically more interesting, however, is how her pictures represented a parody of Smith's charts. She matched his charts with her hostile pictures, parodying the charts on several counts, implicitly linking the dehumanization of women, clinical coldness toward women, and maybe even violence against women (since Smith's women were beheaded) with those arguing for the "partial-birth abortion" ban.

There may be still another example of passive varidirectional double-voiced discourse. Many opposed to the bill argued that the women involved and their physicians should decide what medical procedures are appropriate. Hiding beneath the surface of this argument concerning who should decide was another: that the women in the Senate—not the men—ought to decide the fate of this and similar pieces of legislation. Moseley-Braun noted that, "I never cease to find it a little amusing—I know this gets on some difficult ground in these debates, but most of this debate takes place with people who themselves have never been pregnant" (S 18081). New Jersey's Frank Lautenberg made the same argument at greater length:

The interesting thing to me, Mr. President, is I have not heard one woman speak for that side. It is the men who speak on what women ought to do, tell them how to conduct their lives, tell them what to do with their bodies, describe the pain that they will never feel. It is quite interesting. They want to tell everybody what the moral right is. (S 18197)

Wyoming's Alan Simpson concurred. Speaking "as a man—not a legislator," he says, "I cannot presume to limit the options of any woman who is anguishing over a crisis pregnancy." He goes further: "I do not think a man should even vote on this issue" (S 18225). The women—none of whom spoke for the ban—of course did not really think the men would decline to vote. Rather, they—and male allies—were attempting to make a point about inappropriate male direction on matters so very personal to women.

These uses of passive varidirectional double-voiced discourse suggests carnivalesque energy—insofar as they privilege the position of an oppressed group. So do two other dimensions of the debate. First, the solidarity shown by those supporting Boxer and her position provided a subversive energy. Colleagues came to her assistance when she, exhausted, needed it. They, one-by-one, added their names as supporters to her amendment. Furthermore, they celebrated their solidarity even when they lost. Boxer twice told her colleagues that she was "very moved by the vote that we had" and thanked her "colleagues who stood with . . . me, and with those who feel so strongly about this, that we must put a woman's face on this debate" (S 18199). Feinstein responded, in solidarity, by "commend[ing] my friend and colleague, the junior Senator from California" for being "quite eloquent" throughout the debate (S 18224). Second, the manner in which Boxer (and others) insisted on transforming what might have been an abstract discussion of medical procedures into one that foregrounded women's faces, bodies, and stories insinuated the body into the authorized discourse in a manner reminiscent of the more folk carnivalesque. The contrast between Smith's anatomical charts, which beheaded and objectified the body, and Boxer's photographs, which presented "real" people suggests the different ways in which the two sides introduced the body as well as how Boxer's subversion revealed the dehumanizing assumptions of Smith.

Again, we need to ask if this example of the carnivalesque is illusory—regulated subversiveness in order to thwart genuine subversiveness. Again, the answer is implicit in the extent to which the men arguing in favor of the ban did not "get it." Smith became frustrated at Boxer's failure to respond to his argument that the stories she was reading, although poignant, were irrelevant. He (and others) also seemed awkwardly caught in a bind: they had to acknowledge how moving the stories were. To do otherwise would have been callous and bad politics. However, to the extent they offered this acknowledgement, they undercut the effectiveness of their argument that the stories should be discounted. It is difficult to validate and invalidate simultaneously.

Furthermore, by the time the subtext became apparent, Smith was too emotionally caught up in the debate to respond well. He simply asserted that the law is clear, overlooking what medical practitioners had said their gut response to the law was. Smith also allowed his emotions to boil over when he sarcastically attacked Boxer for not accepting the Dole amendment and offering her own:

It is rather curious, is it not, that throughout the Senate's debate on this bill, the other side has repeatedly demanded a life-of-the-mother exception—repeatedly demanded a life-of-the-mother exception. Yet, when we offer one, we get praised for it, then the gears are switched and we are denounced. . . . This is bizarre. I mean it really is bizarre. I have been involved in a lot of debates. I have served in the Congress for 11 years—I served in the Senate for 5 and the House for 6—and I have been involved in debates on everything. You name it, I have debated it here somewhere. But I do not think I have ever heard a statement that was as quick a turnaround in the same debate as that. (S 18073)

He then proceeded to repeatedly attack the Boxer amendment as a veiled attempt "to gut this bill" (S 18073) and declared "The Senate will not be fooled" (S 18074). He relied increasingly on emotional display, rather than argumentation. For example, he asked, "Stabbing an innocent, tiny baby through the skull and sucking her brains out—how can you justify that?" (S 18075). And he concluded his speaking on the debate's third day by saying, "I urge my colleagues, I plead, plead, plead with my colleagues one time, let us end this one, horrible, disgusting type of abortion" (S 18075).

Just as Boxer perhaps did not argue well early in the debate, he did not argue well here. And, I am suggesting, Boxer's stubborn repetition may have been strategic whereas his simplistic response was not.

The best example of the failure of the men who favored the ban to grasp what was happening involved not Senator Smith but Pennsylvania Senator Rick Santorum. Santorum, fairly late in the debate, lost his composure in the face of Boxer's gallery of photographs. He spoke against them and Boxer's strategy with sarcasm, with anger:

I think what we have trouble with sometimes, as Republicans, is we put up charts, graphs, and numbers, and people just sort of glaze over. On the other side, they are much smarter. There is Senator Boxer with pictures of happy faces. There are no facts and figures. There is no medical evidence to support that partial-birth abortion is the right thing to do, this is the moral thing to do, that this is what our society should stand for. No, you put up pictures of happy, smiling faces. You pull at the heartstrings on the other side and hope that all the truth just gets pushed in the background. (S 18188)

Santorum not only failed to "get it," but expressed a lack of sympathy toward the women pictured that could come back to haunt him. Boxer responded by characterizing his remarks—correctly or incorrectly—as "the most outrageous thing I have ever heard" (S 18188), leading to "tense" interaction between the two as the debate neared its end.

The Senators favoring the ban did not seem to be controlling the carnivalesque energy. Rather, they seemed baffled by it. They were not, however, without their own uses of varidirectional passive double-voiced discourse. They, especially early in the debate, referred to physicians who had performed the procedure in question as "abortionists." When citing these physicians' testimony, the Senators said that the physicians "confessed" various things. The Senators' words both identified people and actions *and* conveyed a negative attitude toward them. Beneath the neutral surface, then, there was a hostile voicing that belied the neutrality. Boxer made an issue of their word choice early in the debate:

> I want to say to my friends on the other side who are leading the charge for criminalizing a medical procedure, that doctors who perform abortions are doctors. They are not abortionists. They are physicians. Many of them have saved women's lives. And you call them abortionists?
>
> Abortion is legal in this country. They are doctors who perform abortions. They are being harassed. They are being threatened. This kind of rhetoric on this floor adds to the problem. A case in point: My colleague said Dr. So-and-so confessed that he performed abortions. He confessed. Notice the word. Who confesses? Somebody who is guilty of a crime. Abortion is not a crime in this Nation. (S 17887)

She repeated her charge late in the debate:

> Now, another thing that has happened over the past few nights—I say to my friend from New Hampshire, he and I have done this now running, I think it is 3 nights running, plus we did it before when this first came up, plus we have been on national television debating each other on this—he uses the term "abortionist." He uses the term "abortionist." . . . If you want to make abortion illegal, that is your right. That is your right. I applaud that right. But do not do it through the backdoor like this, and do not call a doctor who performs a legal procedure an abortionist. (S 18082)

Simpson picked up on another "curious" word choice not in the debaters' words but in those of the bill itself:

> This bill also uses a term I have never before seen in the statute, and I have been doing this for 30 years. Anyone who knowingly performs a partial-birth abortion "and thereby kills a human fetus." That is what it says. "Abortion is thereby killing." (S 18225)

This phraseology, Simpson argues, is "a manifestation of a manipulative group trying to desperately knock off *Roe v. Wade*" (S 18225).

These words implicitly voiced a doctrinaire pro-life position. This implicit position, although consonant with the Senators' arguments in favor of a ban, pulled the debate in a direction they did not, explicitly at least, want it to go in—toward advocacy of a more comprehensive ban. When Senators DeWine and Smith denied this larger goal, one suspects, however, that they may have been ingenuine:

> DEWINE: Some of the opponents of the bill would have the Members of this Senate and the American people believe that this debate is about whether we ban all abortions. It is said that this bill is really not about partial-birth abortion, that what it really is is a covert assault on the decision in *Roe versus Wade*. This is totally false. (S 17895)

> SMITH: We have all heard the debate on abortion. . . . This is a debate that we have had on the Senate floor, and everyone knows where I come from on it. That is not the debate we are having on the Senate floor right now. (S 17900)

> DEWINE: Mr. President, the debate will go on. We will hear again from both sides, but we should try to narrow it and talk about what is at stake. It is not a question of, do we do away with *Roe versus Wade*? . . . It is a very, very, very limited number of abortions that are performed each year. (S 17902)

> SMITH: I have made it very clear, and I think most of my colleagues know that I oppose abortion. I believe abortion takes an innocent human life, no matter what stage of life it is in, whether the day after conception or the day of birth. But that is not the issue today. The issue here is partial-birth abortion. (S 18006)

> SMITH: In spite of the fact that all of us have different opinions about when life begins—and everyone knows my position on that—that is not the issue here, my position on when life begins. That is not relevant today. (S 18008)

SMITH: I want my colleagues to understand—and they all know my position on abortion. I believe life begins at conception and that life is sacred and should be protected. But that is not what we are debating today. . . . That [partial-birth abortion] is what we are talking about, nothing else. Do not be confused by the debate on something else because that is not what we are talking about. (S 18074)

DEWINE: Time and time again on this floor the argument has been made that if you support this bill, it is an attack on *Roe versus Wade*. I would submit that flies in the face of any rational discussion about what *Roe versus Wade* really means and a correct interpretation of it. . . . So this is not an attack on *Roe versus Wade*. You simplistically could argue that. But I think it is very, very incorrect. (S 18085)

LACK OF FINALIZABILITY

One will, of course, never know to what extent the Senators most strongly advocating a ban, had a broader ban in mind. Certainly not all who voted for a ban had this hidden agenda. And there were enough such votes so that Boxer and her allies lost the debate that concluded on December 7. However, that debate, from a Bakhtinian perspective, is but a fragment of a never-finalized polyphony. What did Boxer and her allies then gain in the context of the larger, ongoing debate?

They voiced their concerns that women's reproductive rights, as articulated in *Roe v. Wade*, not be eroded. They made it clear that they were watching for all assaults on these rights. They also attracted to their side many colleagues. Smith repeatedly described the specific medical procedure he claimed the bill was written to outlaw:

> So this specific abortion method called partial-birth abortion—that is what it is called—it is a straightforward, plain English term for a procedure in which a living baby's body is brought entirely into the birth canal, except for the child's head, which the abortionist holds inside the mother's womb, in other words, keeps the child from coming completely out of the womb, restrains the child, keeping the head inside the womb before he punctures the baby's head with scissors and inserts a suction catheter inside that incision and literally sucks the brains out of the child. (S 17885)

If one reads about this particular procedure, one will find it difficult to imagine forty-four Senators taking the risk that a future opponent will read

Smith's words and say the incumbent voted for allowing the procedure. Many Senators then were sufficiently persuaded by the subtext in the debate—that is that the proposed ban was part of a larger assault on women's reproductive freedom—to take that political risk. That there were so many suggests that it will not be just Boxer and other women watching for assaults on the reproductive rights of women. And, although there may indeed be more watching, the number willing to cast the risky vote seems to have shrunk as the unfinalizable debate continued on after December 7. As I am revising this chapter in the Fall of 1999, the matter has again come before the Senate. A bill introduced by Senator Santorum, similar to the one introduced in 1997 by Smith, drew only thirty-four negative votes. The arguments on both sides were similar, as were many of the voices (Dewar, "Late-Term": A4). The sixty-three vote tally in favor of the bill this time—on October 22, 1999—was only four shy of enough to overcome President Clinton's promised veto.

Chapter Six

Southern Senators Resist

Bormann, writing in 1962, analyzes a noteworthy March 1960 debate on a civil rights issue. It was, as I noted in Chapter One, noteworthy because of the quality of the debating several Southern Senators engaged in while filibustering as well as because of their strategy. Just a few days more than a month earlier, there was another debate on a civil rights issue—the poll tax used, allegedly, in some Southern states to deter African Americans from registering to vote. For several days in late January and early February, 1960, several Southern Senators resisted an attempt to declare such a tax illegal. They did not filibuster per se, but the debate nonetheless had many of the characteristics of a filibuster. In this and in other ways, the debate may have served as a trial run for the March debate Bormann analyzed.

VOICES

The matter under consideration was a constitutional amendment introduced by Senator Estes Kefauver of Tennessee to fill temporary vacancies in the House of Representatives in the event of a nuclear catastrophe. To that resolution, Senator Spessard Holland of Florida and sixty-six cosponsors wanted to add a second clause declaring a poll tax unconstitutional. The debate began with Holland—joined occasionally by Lyndon Johnson of Texas and Francis Case of South Dakota—offering a rationale for the proposed second clause. Then Jacob Javits of New York spoke. He objected to the constitutional strategy Holland was using to eliminate the poll tax and proposed, by way of amendment, a law banning the tax.

At that point, a string of Southern Senators took over. Sometimes they spoke against the Javits proposal; sometimes the Holland. Eventually, the two merged into a single focal point for the Southerners' attack. Senators A. Willis Robertson of Virginia, James Eastland of Mississippi, Lister Hill of Alabama, John Sparkman of Alabama, Richard Russell of Georgia, John Stennis of Mississippi, and Olin Johnston of South Carolina all spoke at considerable length against the notion of banning the poll tax, either by constitutional amendment or statute. Supporters of a ban were silent.

The Holland amendment finally passed 72–16, with the Southerners not too disconsolate, for it would require House approval and, then, ratification by the States before it became "law." Javits then pushed for a vote on his proposal, since, in theory, one could ban the poll tax both ways. Javits' amendment was, however, tabled by a vote of 50–37. Then, in an anticlimactic denouement, Paul Douglas of Illinois spoke briefly on why he had supported Javits' amendment. Then, Hubert Humphrey of Minnesota noted his concurrence with Douglas' remarks. These two Senators spoke briefly and after the fact; Javits spent a great deal of his time and energy arguing that a legislative solution was superior to a constitutional one, not indicting the poll tax. Thus, the debate featured very little by way of argumentation against the tax once Holland concluded his restrained opening speech. The debate was the Southerners' opportunity to resist the inevitable. I say "inevitable" for Holland's amendment had sixty-seven sponsors—the precise number needed to bring a filibuster to an end should the Southerners choose that route. They did not, but they certainly did speak at considerable length, perhaps practicing for filibusters to come, including, of course, the one a month and a few days away.

How Holland spoke is worth considering, as is how the Southerners—collectively and individually—spoke. In the Southerners' speeches, much may be implied about arguments that are functioning in the debate without ever having been vocalized. How Javits spoke is also worth considering, for his voice is a rather discordant one. The fact that it was so but nonetheless attracted support may have suggested to the Southerners that, next debate, they could filibuster and defeat a civil rights motion by setting liberals such as Javits against more moderate pro-civil rights Senators.

INTER-VOICES

Holland offered a scholarly indictment of the poll tax. He was rarely if ever emotional; rather, he reviewed the legal facts, as he saw them. He introduced a variety of voices—constitutional scholars, former Senators, reports submitted to the Senate, and the Constitution itself. He proceeded at a good

clip: he did not bog down in a discussion of federal court cases, state constitutions, and the like; and he tended to cite, not quote, the voices he introduced. His presentation was efficient and as noninflammatory as possible.
For example, he demonstrated that in Florida, when the poll tax was elimi-
nated, the registration of both white and black voters increased. He implied
that the poll tax restricted suffrage but not in a racially discriminatory manner:

> It is certainly sound to conclude that the removal of the poll tax re-
> quirement allowed and encouraged many white citizens to vote who
> had not been voting in earlier elections when the poll tax requirement
> applied. . . . A rise from 20,000 to 152,675 in that period of time [1944
> to 1959], and without any great increase in the Negro population of
> Florida, shows clearer than any words the result of banning the
> poll-tax requirement. It is quite clear, Mr. President, that repeal of the
> poll-tax requirement in our State has brought about largely increased
> voting by both the white and colored citizens. (S 1518–19)

Holland's numbers suggested that the effect of repeal was far greater on African Americans than on whites. However, a 1944 repeal of the law banning
Black participation in primaries also had its effects in the post-1943 period.
This repeal allowed Holland to avoid drawing the conclusion that the poll
tax had denied suffrage in a racially discriminatory manner.

Holland was also quite careful to pluralize his voice, so that the case he
presented became not just his. He noted that he "was joined in this Congress
in cosponsoring this proposed constitutional amendment by sixty-six other
Senators" (S 1516). He began arguments with statements such as "We sponsors of Senate Joint Resolution 126 strongly believe" (S 1516).

Before the Southerners took the floor, Javits spoke. Like Holland, he
tended to cite authorities, not quote them, giving his speech a fast pace. But
his tone differed from that of Holland. Rather than create the illusion of objectivity by using data, Javits used emotionally-laden language to indict the
poll tax. For example, Javits argued that "the poll tax is an incubus which
should no longer be carried on the body politic of the American people" (S
1527). In addition, no sense of pluralization was communicated by Javits'
words. In fact, rather than situating himself as spokesperson for many, the
Republican New York Senator suggested that he is balking at the decisions
made by the leadership of the Democratic Party:

> I repeat, I am at a loss to understand why so important a matter as a
> constitutional amendment to eliminate the poll tax and its alterna-
> tive . . . should not be considered and debated on its own. I am at a loss
> to understand why it has to be fastened on as a tail to a joint resolu-
> tion. . . . I must leave the decision on that score, of course, to the leader-
> ship of the majority, but I wish to make it plain to them and to the
> country that I do not consider that the pending amendment to the joint
> resolution does otherwise than complicate the matter. (S 1521)

Javits bristled at the suggestion that he was obstructing the carefully orchestrated plan to eliminate the poll tax: "The Senator from New York is not en-
deavoring to obstruct anything, and he would appreciate it if he were not
accused of it." He also bristled at the suggestion that he was rather late
jumping on the cause and, as a latecomer, ought to be following the plan. He
said, "I should like to say also that Jack Dalton on a white horse, so far as my
reading and my seeing moving pictures is concerned, has never been de-
graded as a hero by the American people simply because he arrived at the
last moment" (S 1524). Javits presented himself as ready to fight. He noted
that, "The Senator from New York is not thin-skinned, and can fight this battle without these characterizations." He further noted that, although Holland is known to be "a good, tough fighter," he, Javits, is "not overwhelmed"
and is "perfectly ready to take on the test of debate and the test of authorities" (S 1524). His weaponry will be cited and quoted evidence, it seemed;
and—and this is important—his opponent will be not those defending the
poll tax but, rather, Senator Holland who was advocating its elimination by
a different mechanism.

Javits seemed in the debate to be largely alone. However, do note that
both Douglas and Humphrey retroactively supported him. Also note that his
cause will attract thirty-seven votes in the end. That roster, including names
such as Clifford Case of New Jersey, Philip Hart of Michigan, Vance Hartke
of Indiana, Kenneth Keating of New York, Thomas Kuchel of California,
Eugene McCarthy of Minnesota, Wayne Morse of Oregon, Edmund
Muskie of Maine, and William Proxmire of Wisconsin, has a pronounced
liberal tinge. As I noted earlier, Javits' discordant presence and the liberal
support he, albeit quietly, received in this debate may have suggested to the
Southerners that a moderate-liberal schism was possible in the pro-civil
rights rank.

The seven Southern Senators who spoke at length were not as parsimoni-
ous when it came to evidence use as Holland and Javits. Whereas the two
poll tax opponents tended to cite rather than quote, the Southerners quoted

extensively and exhaustively. If the task were to review early state constitutions on the matter of voting qualifications, they would review every state's; if the task were to summarize federal court decisions relevant to the poll tax, they would review every court case. It is this exhaustiveness that gave the Southerners' speeches the feel of a filibuster.

Bormann argued that in the March 1960 debate the different Southern Senators had—it seemed—assigned roles: Sam Ervin of North Carolina on the legal; Harry Byrd of Virginia on the constitutional; Holland of Florida on the practical; and Eastland of Mississippi on the moral. In the January–February 1960 debate, a different group exhibited—it seemed—a lesser degree of specialization. That specialization was noticeable in the kinds of evidentiary voices they cited or quoted. Sparkman of Alabama, Russell of Georgia, Stennis of Mississippi, and Johnston of South Carolina offered a range of voices. However, Robertson of Virginia specialized in citing or quoting federal court decisions; Eastland of Mississippi specialized in citing or quoting state constitutions and state laws from the 18th century to the 20th; and Hill of Alabama specialized in citing or quoting what those associated with the federal Constitutional Convention and the related state conventions had said. Hill also specialized in quoting past presidents.

One can learn a great deal from reading these Senators' lengthy presentations. As in the March 1960 filibuster, they did not read from the Washington, DC telephone directory. Rather, they offered scholarly arguments. They were tedious only because these arguments were so extensive and so exhaustive. The scholarly quality of their accounts—supported, one would imagine, by much homework on the part of their aides—anticipated a similar quality in the March 1960 debate that Bormann studied.

There were, however, a few interesting breaks from the cited and quoted voices of authorities these Southern Senators offered. Robertson engaged in a kind of stylization. Referring to Javits' remarks, Robertson said, "Although he is a brilliant lawyer, I feel he gave a demonstration today of the old maxim, 'There are none so blind as they that won't see.' " Robertson repeats the "maxim" in a colloquy with Russell, asking if the Georgia Senator agreed. Russell responded, "That saying is as old as Holy Writ, and I will be the last to dispute it" (S 1529). The allusion is perhaps to Isaiah 43:8 or Jeremiah 5:21, filtered through Matthew Henry. But regardless of source, the voice adds dignity and weight—if not divine blessing—to the cause Robertson is defending. Robertson also quotes his colleague Javits' "incubus" remark several times. He does not play off of the obscure term's sexual connotations; rather, he seems to be making fun of its obscurity and its humorous sound when spoken aloud (especially with a Southern accent). Robertson seems to be parodying Javits, the point of which is to satirize the specific comment and, by extension, mute all of the New York Senator's arguments.

Stennis added variety to the voices, if nothing else. He stylized Portia's often-recited (by ninth graders) speech in Shakespeare's *The Merchant of Venice* by saying that, "The privileges we enjoy simply do not come like rain from heaven" (S 1717). He interjected the everyday by quoting signs such as "Shelter. Safety Here" (S 1716) and "nothing down and a dollar a month" (S 1717). He imagined a football coach saying, "We are going to make a touchdown, but we are going only 90 yards; we will move the goal line" (S 1719). He also quoted a—perhaps imaginary—constituent:

> I was greatly shocked not too long ago when a very intelligent woman said to me, in Washington, "Why not abolish the States, anyway? Why do we need them any longer." (S 1679)

The rhetorical effect of these less scholarly voices is, perhaps, best assessed by lumping them together. Stennis, unlike his peers, is trying to humanize the debate somewhat. Perhaps the average voter will understand the significance of changing what the Constitution says about election rules—and who sets them—by considering the analogy of changing the rules of a football game. Perhaps the average voter will understand the abstract issue of "states' rights" by considering the woman's question for a few minutes. If nothing else, Stennis' other voices provide some relief after hours—days—of cited and quoted authorities.

DOUBLE-VOICING AND CARNIVALESQUE

If one merges all of what the Southern Senators say in opposition to both Holland's and Javits' amendments, the Southerners are arguing the following: (1) that the poll tax is not a significant barrier to registering because the dollar amount per capita is so small; (2) that the tax is levied in a nondiscriminatory manner; (3) that the revenue gathered by the poll tax is necessary for education; (4) that the poll tax is vanishing on its own; and (5) that the poll tax, as well as other voter qualifications, is a state not a federal concern. Two of these arguments seem to be voiced with unusual emphasis—the second and the fifth. It is as if the proposed legislation hit two nerves, the discrimination nerve and the states' rights nerve.

Words, phrases, and utterances all have entailments—entailments tied to their prior uses. Sometimes these entailments are rhetorically relevant, sometimes not. In this particular case, they are. Both Holland and Javits refrained from accusing "The South" of discrimination. Holland argued that the poll tax denied suffrage but on a nondiscriminatory basis. Javits argued that his proposed amendment was directed at all barriers to suffrage, including many in "The North." Both Holland and Javits avoided the question of jurisdiction, except, peripherally, in discussing whether a constitutional amendment is necessary to effect the prohibition. Despite their care, with the very topic of banning the poll tax came entailments from its previous discussions. And, during those previous discussions—in and out of the legislature, the accusation of racial discrimination and the assault on what the Southerners saw as their states' rights were more prominent. Note that the principal—almost sole—speaker against the poll tax was a Southerner, a Senator who, ironically, would join the Southern Senators in filibustering in March. Holland's being a Southerner did not, however, curtail the entailments from becoming a moving force in the poll tax debate.

The result of these unvocalized entailments playing a role in the debate is a kind of double-voiced discourse. The Senators arguing against the poll tax voice certain arguments. Because of the contexts in which those arguments have previously been used, other voices join in—never voiced per se, but nonetheless functioning in the debate. These voices made the objectionable arguments that Southern states had used the poll tax to discriminate against African Americans and that the federal government knew how to—and should—dictate the electoral affairs of recalcitrant Southern states. Because these entailments are not under the control of these Senators, this double-voiced discourse is actually, in Bakhtin's terms, active, not passive.

The "evidence" of these "silent" voices functioning in the debate is the Southerner Senators' responses. They defended "states' rights" strongly. Often, they addressed the issue directly. For example, Johnston of South Carolina observed that, "Whether or not any individual Senator believes the payment of a poll tax should or should not be a qualification for voting has nothing to do with the underlying principle which is at stake here today." That principle, he went on to note, was "the right of States to control their own election machinery and to set forth qualifications which citizens must meet before they are eligible to vote" (S 1744). Sometimes, they used the genre of colloquy to make the point that all is well under a system of "states' rights":

SPARKMAN: Is it not true that an examination of the statutes of the several States of the Union today shows a great lack of uniformity not only with reference to the subject presently under consideration, the poll tax, but also as to other subjects, such as the length of time a person must live in a State, in a county, or in a precinct; property taxes; and whether the person is a pauper? Some States decline to register paupers. Many other things indicate a great lack of anything like uniformity.

HILL: The Senator is exactly correct. There were varying requirements to qualify one to be an elector in the several States.

SPARKMAN: Dependent upon what the States respectively decided?

HILL: That is correct.

SPARKMAN: Each State for itself?

HILL: Each State in its own full and complete and absolute sovereignty made its own decisions as to the qualifications of electors. (S 1612)

In response to the unvoiced accusation of the racial discrimination, they responded in two ways—defensively and offensively. A good example of the defensive was Russell's comment that

> Every day some of our friends from other parts of the Nation examine the Southern States with a magnifying glass—in an attempt to find some flyspeck which, when magnified, might look as large as Stone Mountain. If they find something, they say: "Look at what the Southerners are doing." Then they run to Washington and complain about it. (S 1660)

Examples of the offensive were found in the many indictments the Southerners offered of election practices in "The North." For example, Robertson said that Javits' "incubus" remark "reminded me of a reference in a speech against a poll tax bill in August of 1948, in which I referred to a qualification of the State of New York known as the literacy test" (S 1529). At greater length, Robertson later noted that, "Some eighteen States have other forms of literacy requirements as a prerequisite to voting eligibility." He cited Connecticut as an example, in which "in order to be qualified for voting one must be able to read any article of the U.S. Constitution or any section of the Connecticut statutes in the English language" (S 1661). At still much greater length, Eastland offered a multipage statement on the issue. He first dealt with restrictions enacted by eighteenth-century state constitutions. He quoted those of Pennsylvania, New York, North Carolina, New Hampshire, Maryland, New Jersey, South Carolina, Massachusetts, Georgia, and Virginia. To the extent these documents restricted suffrage, they validated what he argued was the "Founding Fathers'" intention that such matters as voter qualifications be left to the States. Then, he focused on present restrictions. He began, tongue in cheek, by saying:

Mr. President, I want it clearly understood as I go into this subject that I am not trying to pass any judgments on the wisdom or justice of the laws of any State of the union, save my own, insofar as voting qualifications are concerned. The setting of these qualifications and requirements is peculiarly within the Constitutional rights and privileges of the States themselves. However, the avowed purpose of the proposed constitutional amendment is to throw stones at the State of Mississippi. So as a purely academic exercise I am going to take this occasion to comment on the voting requirements of some of the States and put these in juxtaposition with those of other States. (S 1724)

He examined literacy test requirements in New York, New Mexico, Arizona, California, Alaska, and Hawaii. He looked at intrusive questions asked by different states as part of voter registration. He looked at the oaths new voters are required to swear. He then looked at the twenty-three states that have literacy requirements (as distinct from literacy test requirements). He then examined the nine states that have property requirements. Eastland's point, in this "academic exercise," was to suggest to his Senate peers that they should not throw that stone at Mississippi unless their states are without the sin of restricting suffrage in one way or another. His "stone" remark also is an example of stylization, thereby associating his call for restraint with Jesus Christ's.

Read in 1999, this debate seems not only one-sided in bulk but one-sided in substance. The Southern Senators defending the poll tax held the Senate floor most of the time by offering their well-researched and lengthy addresses. The arguments presented in these speeches seemed sound and were countered by very little by the sixty-seven Senators who were prepared to vote for Holland's resolution. So, why were these sixty-seven Senators sitting by silently ready to cast their vote? Obviously, there were arguments relevant to the debate—compelling ones—that were not being made. In 1999, we cannot "read" them: they are not printed on the page. They were nonetheless present in the debate: they are the entailments that were silently but powerfully voiced when Holland and Javits raised the poll tax issue in a manner that seemed, on the surface, to be inoffensive. How powerful these entailments were in the minds of those voting against the poll tax was apparent in the sixty-seven names attached as cosponsors to Holland's resolution. This curiously unvoiced double-voiced discourse outweighed all the evidence the Southern Senators might have amassed.

The Southern Senators, of course, knew how the vote on Holland's resolution would go. Any bill with sixty-seven cosponsors is certainly going to pass in a legislative body of one hundred. In the face of defeat, they talked on, but the tone of their speeches was far from resigned or forlorn. Rather, they seemed to be having a good time. Their near-filibuster had a celebratory tone, a carnivalesque quality.

They praised each other profusely. Robertson took "this opportunity warmly to commend my distinguished friend, the Senator from Alabama [Hill], for the splendid presentation he is making here this afternoon of a vital principle of constitutional government" (S 1617). Hill then thanked "my distinguished friend [Robertson] and [told] him how deeply I appreciate his words. I particularly appreciate them," Hill added, "inasmuch as they come from one who on yesterday made so magnificent and masterful address on this very subject" (S 1618).

If this "loving" exchange strikes you as just an exaggeration of usual Senate courtesy, consider how effusive Hill is and how much fun he is having in the following:

> I yield to my distinguished friend, the Senator from the great state of Virginia, which gave to the Nation the great James Madison. On yesterday, the Senator from Virginia made in this Chamber a speech that was so masterful that I did not hesitate to say that I feel that if Mr. Madison and some of the other Founding Fathers from Virginia could then have been in the Senate galleries, they would have been proud of the Senator from Virginia. So I take pleasure in yielding to him. (S 1611)

The celebratory, carnivalesque tone is also apparent in many of the colloquies the Southern Senators staged. For example, early in the debate, Herman Talmadge of Georgia and Robertson of Virginia talked about "states' rights":

TALMADGE: Does the Senator believe that the Congress has demonstrated any superior knowledge as to how the affairs of Virginia or Oregon should be conducted, as compared with the knowledge possessed by the General Assembly of Virginia or of the State of Oregon?

ROBERTSON: Of course, the States can handle their domestic affairs better than can the Central Government in Washington. . . . Certainly the Congress has not shown any superior wisdom over that of the States in conducting the domestic affairs of the country.

TALMADGE: Does not the distinguished Senator feel that the legislatures of the 50 States of the Union are closer to the people, and are better qualified to judge what laws they should have regarding their election machinery, than any agency that operates through compulsion, be it by means of a constitutional amendment, legislation, or otherwise, from Washington, DC?

ROBERTSON: I could not agree more completely. . . .

TALMADGE: Is it not true that the more remote government is from the people, the less responsive it is to the will of the people?

ROBERTSON: The Senator is absolutely correct.

TALMADGE: Is it not true that when we centralize all regulatory power in the Central Government, far removed from the people, that is the beginning of dictatorship, under which the people cannot control the Government, but rather are controlled by the Government?

ROBERTSON: The Senator is correct. The great bulwark against any drift into socialism, and eventually from socialism into dictatorship, is the rights of the 50 sovereign States. (S 1534)

The carnivalesque is apparent throughout the Southerners' near-filibuster. In fact, I would suggest that a filibuster, by definition, is a carnivalesque moment. Filibusters are used by a minority to subvert authority. Once the filibuster is underway, power is in a sense temporarily reversed; for the disempowered minority, as long as it can hold the floor, has become empowered. A filibuster furthermore foregrounds the body—not in Rabelais' manner, but insofar as the bodies of those filibustering hold the floor and, perhaps, acquire the rankness of the hours or days of endless debate.

What perhaps made the filibuster in the cases of civil rights bills seem not especially carnivalesque is how much power the Southern Senators involved in the filibustering had in the Senate. Many were quite senior, holding Committee chairmanships and, therefore, able to determine the fates of bills—and junior members' careers. Nonetheless, on civil rights matters, they were clearly a minority. As Russell noted,

It is seldom a comfortable feeling to be in a hopeless minority. It is even less comfortable to face a majority which includes many good friends and staunch allies in other important, hard-fought battles. That, unhappily, is the painful predicament in which I find myself today. It is a predicament from which there is no escape. (S 1659)

The tone of Russell's comment is rather sad. The tone suggests that he sees himself in the minority not just on a matter of policy but on the more important issue of one's way of life. The abolition of the poll tax per se is not what threatens Russell's way of life, especially since his state, Georgia, had abolished the tax in 1945. Rather, entailed within the calmly offered indictments of the poll tax is the unvoiced assault on the South and the right of the states in the South to be as they want to be. It is what Russell foresees as the inevitable victory of this unvoiced assault that makes him seem such a sad member of "a hopeless minority." Beneath the joviality of his Southern colleagues' carnivalesque filibuster perhaps lurks a similar sadness. And, insofar as the sixty-seven who could invoke cloture are allowing the near-filibuster to proceed, this example of carnivalesque does seem licensed. Keep in mind, however, that these Southern Senators will filibuster a month and a few days later, and it will not be a licensed disruption of authority then.

LACK OF FINALIZABILITY

Bormann's analysis of that March filibuster serves as a reminder that the debate over the poll tax did not really end with the vote to approve Holland's resolution and table Javits' amendment. The debate, defined broadly as the argumentation surrounding various attempts to guarantee African Americans the full rights of citizenship throughout the nation, did not end with the March 1960 debate either. There would be many other civil rights debates in the years ahead. Some of these debates would spill outside the walls of the Senate Chamber. Demonstrations, rallies, imprisonments, and even assassinations would become parts of an unfinalizable dialogue. Even after the passage of several landmark civil rights laws, the dialogue did not end. Recent discussions of race relations in the aftermath of the criminal and civil trials of O. J. Simpson as well as recent challenges to affirmative action mandates demonstrate that the discussion continues. Both in the temporal sense and in the strategic sense, this early 1960 debate continues on.

Chapter Seven

Senators Reject Clement Haynsworth

In the previous case studies, I have analyzed Senate debates much in the same manner. Following the heuristic procedure outlined in Chapter Two, I have identified the voices in the debates; considered the inter-voices these speakers interject; noted instances of double-voiced discourse and the carnivalesque; and at least addressed the unfinalizable nature of the debates under scrutiny. A written analysis that derives from this Bakhtinian heuristic, however, need not proceed in that step-by-step manner. Sometimes, the analysis can more accurately represent the contours of the debate if it proceeds more narratively. Such is the case for the lengthy, rather shapeless debate over President Richard M. Nixon's nomination of Clement F. Haynsworth, Jr., to be an Associate Justice of the U.S. Supreme Court. In examining this November 1969 debate, I will take the reader through it day by day, looking through all of the lenses of the Bakhtinian paradigm as I go. I will also deal, when relevant, with Vatz and Windt's 1974 *Quarterly Journal of Speech* essay on the Haynsworth and the later Carswell nominations, an essay that, as I indicated in Chapter One, misanalyzes at least the first debate, although that analysis is alert to some of the dynamics of the five-day event.

Vatz and Windt offer as a critical observation what some of Haynsworth's defenders, in and out of the Senate, said about the debating of at least some members of the loose coalition of opposing Senators. Supposedly, the objection to Haynsworth's nomination was based on either his ethical lapses or his failure to be sufficiently concerned about the appearance of ethical lapses. Supposedly, this objection was but a smoke screen, veiling the true objections. As newspaper columnist James J. Kilpatrick put the matter,

What we are witnessing, in the trumped-up "case against Haynsworth," is a triumph of the propagandist's craft. Into a smoking pot, the judge's opponents have flung a shrewd mixture of truth, half-truth, whole lies, base insinuations, and old-fashioned politics. By heating up this far-rago, they have created great clouds of unfounded doubt; and they have succeeded in making this phony doubt the very basis of their opposition. . . . When the record is seen clearly, and not through a smokescreen, the record discloses not even the appearance of impropriety. The trouble is that the smokescreen is so thick that busy men—and Senators are busy men—cannot conveniently take the time to penetrate the fog. (S 34859)

These true objections, hidden behind the fog, were tied, according to Vatz and Windt, to Haynsworth's record as a jurist on civil rights and labor cases. Several Senators found that record objectionable in its own right for it seemed to tolerate segregation and union busting. Furthermore, they worried about the judicial philosophy implicit in the decisions that comprised that record. This "reading" of the debate would lead one to expect that matters of ethics would be discussed at length while Haynsworth's civil rights and labor record would be, perhaps, mentioned in passing. Well, the debate does not match this description at all: all three issues are very much present throughout the debate. The civil rights and labor relations decisions were not hidden.

DAY ONE

Senators James Eastland of Mississippi and Roman Hruska of Nebraska began the debate, presenting their case for the confirmation of Judge Clement Haynsworth. They cited authorities; they quoted authorities; they also cited and quoted fellow Senators. What is obvious in their presentation is that we are, in a sense, beginning *in medias res*. Well-publicized hearings have already been held, but, even before those committee hearings, some opponents began preparing for their assault. For example, Senator Birch Bayh's lengthy list of ethical objections, which the Indiana Senator prepared prior to the publication of the Judiciary Committee's majority report, was referred to by both Eastland and Hruska. Eastland raised the NAACP's already-stated objections; Hruska raised the AFL–CIO's. Although occasionally refuting these charges, both Eastland and Hruska adhered to generic expectations and began the debate with the case for Haynsworth, including the expected parade of endorsements.

Senator Bayh spoke next. He did indeed focus on the ethical questions. In brief, he believed that Judge Haynsworth should have excused himself from hearing several cases because of conflicts of interest. The array of voices Bayh used was quite similar to that used by Eastland and Hruska except that Bayh often cited federal law (specifically, 28 USC 455) and the several canons of judicial ethics endorsed by the American Bar Association (ABA) that Haynsworth allegedly violated.

Beginning here—and continuing throughout the entire debate—was a battle over sources. The battle was not over who has the better sources; rather, the battle was over who—that is, which side—"owns" a particular source. The battle was fought over the legal scholars and historians who testified before the Senate Judiciary Committee. Each side, to the extent there were sides, wanted to bask in the aura of the source's credentials and supposed objectivity. The battle was also fought over the meaning of federal court decisions Haynsworth authored or coauthored, Haynsworth's dissenting opinions, and the Supreme Court opinions that reversed or confirmed these lower court decisions. Sometimes, the debate sounded more like that which would occur in a law school classroom than in the Senate chamber.

Senator Marlow Cook of Kentucky spoke after Bayh. To the extent he discussed the objections to Haynsworth's ratification, he focused on the alleged ethical lapses. This focus made sense, since he was speaking after Bayh. Cook also presented an historical review of rejected Supreme Court nominees. He tried to suggest to his peers that rejection is rare and therefore the Senate ought to go along with Nixon—barring any serious ethical problems:

[T]he Senate has in its past almost without exception objected to nominees for the Supreme Court for political reasons. There were times, however, when it sought to hide its political objections under the veil of cries about fitness, ethics, and qualifications. This body has, in more recent years, come to the conclusion that the advice and consent responsibility of the Senate should mean an inquiry into qualifications and not politics. Various Senators of liberal persuasion have argued to conservatives in regard to appointments they liked that the ideology of the nominee was not the business of the Senate. I accept that argument. I agree that for the Senate to go back to its habit in the nineteenth century of purely political consideration of nominees to the Supreme Court would degrade the Court and certainly not distinguish the Senate. (S 34269)

Cook's speech concluded with a colloquy between himself and Senator Sam Ervin of North Carolina. During that colloquy, they tried to claim statements by textile union official Patricia Eames and former attorney general Robert Kennedy for the pro-Haynsworth "side." Bayh quickly implied that they were quoting Eames out of context when he asked that her full letter be entered into the record. (The use of Robert Kennedy's statement as evidence will draw a response later in the debate from Bayh.)

Following another colloquy, this time between Cook and Fritz Hollings of South Carolina, Senator Javits took the floor. Javits' objections to Haynsworth were not based on alleged ethical lapses, a matter he says he will leave to others to discuss and decide:

I do not pass on the question of ethics. That has been stated by other Senators. . . . As its determination was not necessary for my decision, I did not make it. That does not mean there is nothing to it. I just found it unnecessary to decide that question "yes" or "no" and I do not feel that I should deal with it in the presentation of my reasons for voting "no" on this confirmation. (S 34275)

Rather, his objections were to the nominee's civil rights record—in particular to what Javits saw as the nominee's failure to embrace the Supreme Court decision in *Brown v Board of Education, Topeka, Kansas* in numerous rulings on school desegregation matters in the 4th Circuit's area. Javits reviewed numerous such rulings. "I think this review demonstrates," he concluded, "that . . . Judge Haynsworth has been consistently in error, systemically and relentlessly opposed to implementation of the Supreme Court's 1954 desegregation decision and consistently sympathetic to every new device for delay" (S 34275).

After he spoke, he and Senator Robert Byrd of West Virginia debated whether or not the Senate should even consider a nominee's positions on issues such as civil rights in offering its advice and consent. Javits quoted several Southern Senators (Strom Thurmond of South Carolina, Sam Ervin of North Carolina, John Stennis of Mississippi) now supporting Haynsworth, quoted Charles Warren's history of the Supreme Court, cited a *Yale Law Journal* article on the matter, and cited a similar *New York Times* article by Anthony Lewis, which he entered into the record. These sources, Javits argued, suggested that the Senate should indeed look at a nominee's judicial record.

Senator B. Everett Jordan of Idaho delivered the last lengthy presentation on the debate's first day (November 13, 1969). In a rather moving speech, he talked about how he, a Republican, did not want to oppose Nixon's nominee but, on the basis of the ethics charge, felt he must. Authorities per se disappeared as inter-voices in Jordan's speech. He quoted and cited Haynsworth. He also referred to the letters and calls his office had received pressuring him to support Nixon:

> During my more than 7 years of service in the U.S. Senate few issues have generated more pressure on my office than has the confirmation of Judge Haynsworth's nomination. Support of the President is urged as if it were a personal matter rather than an issue of grave constitutional importance. . . . [A]dministration calls to my State have been legion. Some of my friends have been persuaded to call me even though they have not been provided copies of the hearing record from which they might make an independent judgment as I have done. (S 34288)

This sparse use of inter-voices and the focus on his personal decision-making gave Jordan's address a different, less scholarly tone from that of the preceding speeches.

DAY TWO

Senator Byrd of West Virginia began the debating on the second day, November 17, 1969. In support of Haynsworth, he refuted the ethics charge *and* the civil rights charge *and* the labor charge. He used what was rapidly becoming the standard array, for this debate, of evidence and evidence types. That Byrd addressed all three indictments of Haynsworth so very early in the debate was a demonstration that all three were very much a part of the case that was being offered against the nominee. The arguments against Haynsworth's judicial positions were not at all hiding behind the ethical challenges.

Similarly broad in its scope was Montana Senator Lee Metcalf's speech. After justifying opposition to a president's choice for the Supreme Court on the basis of a nominee's judicial stands, Metcalf criticized Haynsworth's record on school segregation and labor relations. Unlike others who will speak against the nominee, Metcalf spent more time talking about the labor relations issue. He concluded by briefly criticizing Haynsworth's alleged ethical lapses and by noting how much pressure the Nixon White House was applying on members of the Senate. "The activities of employees on the President's staff are well known," he commented. "Members of the Senate have been threatened, coerced, high pressured, and offered special projects and appointments, all to secure votes for Judge Haynsworth's confirmation" (S 34432).

Senator Howard Baker of Tennessee was the next speaker. In a very lawyer-like fashion, he devoted most of his time to rejecting the allegation that Haynsworth was retrograde on the question of school desegregation. He did so by examining, one by one, the nominee's school-related decisions. His matter-of-fact presentation was interrupted by Senator Robert Dole of Kansas, who introduced into the debate a letter written by former Supreme Court Associate Justice Whittaker. Whittaker indicted the opposition to Haynsworth for hiding its "real" reasons for rejecting the nominee behind a flimsy ethical challenge:

> Inasmuch as there is no support in the record for the charges of unethical conduct that are being widely hurled and publicized against Judge Haynsworth by his opponents, it simply has to be that they are doing these for other reasons—perhaps because they do not like his non-legislative and conservative judicial philosophies, yet do not want frankly to oppose him on their real grounds for fear that to do so would not be politically expedient to them. . . . I simply say that it seems to me to be a shame that his opponents are willing to falsely assault his character in order to obtain his defeat because they want a more "liberal" justice appointed to the Supreme Court. (S 34436)

The debate at this point became more heated as Bayh declared that he was offended at the impugning of his motives by Whittaker and that his objections were philosophical, not crassly political. After Baker and Dole collaborated in keeping Whittaker's voice "heard," Dole offered a fictitious, sarcastic rendition of what AFL–CIO President George Meany might say about any nominee without a "perfect" pro-labor record:

> Some appeared before the committee, for example, George Meany; certainly he is opposed on philosophical grounds. He says in effect "He is antilabor; we are going to block him, just as we did Judge Parker in the Hoover administration." (S 34438)

Dole's prosopopoeia seemed designed to suggest that Bayh's philosophical stance is no more philosophical than the AFL–CIO president's.

Then, Wyoming Senator Clifford Hansen attempted to refute the indictment of Haynsworth's labor record. He drew, as Dole had, an analogy between the nominee and John J. Parker, a previous nominee rejected by the

Senate primarily because of lobbying by organized labor. Just as everyone later came to admit the mistake they had made in the case of Parker, so will everyone eventually come to admit the mistake in the case of Haynsworth, Hansen argued:

Organized labor now concedes that it misjudged its man in 1930, and that its opposition was a mistake. Mr. Thomas Harris, general counsel of the AFL–CIO, stated at the Judiciary Committee hearings on the Haynsworth nomination: "I agree with you that the attack on Judge Parker . . . was unjustified. . . ." More objective observers, feeling that the Supreme Court in the ensuing 39 years could have used the legal talents of John J. Parker, may not feel that the result was quite as funny as Mr. Harris thinks it was. But these observers would doubtless agree with Mr. Harris that the Senate did make a mistake when it refused to confirm the nomination of Judge Parker, of whom Chief Justice Earl Warren said in 1958: "No judge in the land was more fully distinguished or more sincerely loved." I, for one, do not relish the prospect of some future general counsel of the AFL–CIO, or any other organization, telling us 40 years from now that the organization made a mistake in opposing Judge Haynsworth in 1969. (S 34439)

Then, Senator Winston Prouty of Vermont, using a press release, announced he would vote for the nominee. The release says essentially what Whittaker had said—that the "real" objection to Haynsworth is political, not ethical:

The Vermonter said he had studied the record carefully and found that "the blizzard of accusations against Judge Haynsworth melts quickly under close scrutiny. . . ." Prouty found the opposition to Haynsworth to be "more on political grounds than ethical grounds and more emotional than reasoned." (S 34439)

Florida Senator Edward Gurney agreed and commended Senators, such as Javits, who had raised the "real" issues, rather than hide behind the smoke screen of the ethical charges:

[W]e can applaud the candor of those critics of Judge Haynsworth, such as the AFL–CIO, and the National Educational Association—NEA—who have admitted that their objections frankly do go to Judge Haynsworth's judicial record, and not to his stock market dealings. In fact, I commend the senior Senator from New York (Javits), who said that he would not talk about the ethics matter, because he opposed the judge on his attitude toward civil rights matters—in other words, on philosophical grounds. I think he was being very honest and candid in stating that that was what his objection was. (S 34439)

There is clearly confirmation of Vatz and Windt's analysis in what Whittaker, Prouty, and Gurney say. They did seem to characterize the debate as consisting of ethical charges serving as a smoke screen behind which the "real" charges lurk. The problem with this analysis is that these "real" charges were so fully voiced and so fully refuted in the debate that they hardly seemed to be lurking. There were three lines of argument in the debate, not an argument behind which hides two instances of double-voiced discourse. However, there may well have been a different way in which double-voiced discourse functioned in the debate. On the surface, there were the three indictments of Haynsworth; hidden was a political argument indeed. Put in blunt political terms, the argument was to do whatever was necessary to prevent Nixon from altering the tenor of the Supreme Court. All of the arguments against Haynsworth may well at least partially be a smoke screen for this political purpose.

Gurney came close to stating as much. He contextualized the Haynsworth nomination within the 1968 presidential election. He talked about why voters selected Nixon over Humphrey. A chief concern of the people, according to Gurney, was the too-liberal Warren Court. The people elected Nixon to reform the Court:

[A]nother matter which disturbed many people in Florida, and which I found very much in their minds, was the behavior of the Supreme Court on a number of fronts. The people expressed to me dissatisfaction with the course of the Supreme Court's decision on school prayer, and outlawing Bible reading in schools. They were upset with the apportionment decisions which heretofore had been political matters within the exclusive jurisdiction of the States. They were irritated with the Supreme Court's tinkering with and even upsetting some State constitutions. They resented the way in which the court had effectively curbed efforts of law enforcement and postal authorities to stop the flood of pornography. They resented the recent striking down of residency requirements for welfare recipients. They resented the striking down of the marihuana tax control laws. They were upset, and rightfully so, with the seemingly ludicrous criminal decisions such as

Miranda, Escobedo, and a whole string of successive cases. Very often they did not know the names of the decisions. They could not give a citation, or anything of that sort. But they had the feeling, and I think the feeling was correct, that the thrust of many of these opinions was to free criminals, in some cases self-confessed criminals, on the flimsiest sort of technicalities. They expressed to me the view, and it is a view I subscribe to, that in the midst of the greatest crime wave in our Nation's history, the decisions of the court which resulted in the freeing of criminals were absurd, almost, as one constituent told me, "like throwing gasoline on the fire." (S 34440–41)

Wherever Gurney raised the topic of the Supreme Court during the campaign, he noted, "there was a roar such as I cannot describe on the Senate floor. It was a roar of disapproval by the people" (S 34442). A vote against Haynsworth then is a vote against Nixon as the people's designated Court reformer. In making this suggestion, Gurney may have correctly identified the truly hidden argument.

The next major speaker was Virginia Senator William Spong. He focused on the ethical charge, bringing in what are by now the usual sources. Then, Senator Edward Brooke of Massachusetts spoke. Speaking in a restrained, objective manner, Brooke praised the nominee for innovative decisions in criminal law but then expressed reservations about Haynsworth's school desegregation decisions as well as his veracity when testifying before the Senate. Dole then introduced a Chicago *Tribune* article that attacked the AFL–CIO and NAACP positions; then Hruska, relying heavily on Professor G. W. Foster's testimony, defended Haynsworth's civil rights records against Javits' accusations.

DAY THREE

Day Three (November 18, 1969) began with two-and-a-half hours of Senator Fritz Hollings of South Carolina. He began by noting—at length—the union-inspired, media-driven character assassination campaign against Haynsworth. Before refuting, charge by charge, the allegations made by Bayh in his "Bill of Particulars," Hollings brought in another political dimension of the debate. He suggested that opposing Senators saw in the South Carolina jurist's nomination Nixon's paying-off "The South" for its support in the 1968 election:

Throughout, the "southern strategy" of President Nixon was rebuked. With headlines reading, "Haynsworth Selection Seen as Thurmond

Payoff," one witness testified that the appointment was "one of the dirtiest and most sordid political games that has ever been played with judgeships as pawns and poker chips in the history of the Republic. (S 34554)

Haynsworth's nomination then was a final piece of Nixon's "Southern strategy." And Nixon's opponents—Hollings implied—were rejecting Haynsworth to thwart that Southern political strategy. And, when their ethical objections began to disintegrate under scrutiny, these opponents called for the nominee's withdrawal. As Hollings put it in one of the debate's most memorable similes, "The opposition, like the trapped octopus, has darkened the waters of reason with his black ink of poison and escaped, chortling while Senators run in circles shouting 'withdrawal,' 'insensitivity,' 'lack of judgment,' 'shadows,' and 'lack of candor' " (S 34562).

Hollings, in 180 minutes of speaking, introduced many inter-voices. Most were of the sort we have seen already—citations of authorities, quotations of authorities, references to and quotations of colleagues, references to and quotations of himself. Hollings also was a very heavy user of prosopopoeia. He had Haynsworth's opponents saying "We have to get rid of this wheeler-dealer" (S 34554); Bayh yelling "Withdrawal, withdrawal" (S 34555); opponents saying to each other "Do not stop, do not answer, do not discuss, keep on charging; we have him on the run" (S 34560); and opponents of the nominee's civil rights and labor relations records declaring "This thing is disturbing to me. This man has got blinders. He is ruling on civil rights, union, and student matters, as of 10 years ago" (S 34564).

Following Hollings were Baker defending Haynsworth's civil rights record and, then, Javits attacking it. Previously discussed court cases were reviewed, as were new ones. The civil rights issue was certainly being discussed very fully—too fully for it to be considered a veiled matter in the debate. After these speeches, Bayh argued that there was clearly room for disagreement over whether the reasoning in these cases was retrograde or cautious and, then, he tried to return the debate to the ethical charges he had advanced. Bayh also attempted at this point to deny Haynsworth's defenders the late Bobby Kennedy as their "witness." Bayh quoted Senator Edward Kennedy's testimony to the Judiciary Committee as arguing that "[n]owhere either in the allegation that was raised by Patricia Eames or in Judge Sobeloff's records or comments did they ever reach the question about the initial propriety of Judge Haynsworth sitting on that case. . . . The matter that came to the Justice Department was sent to the Criminal Division, referred to the Criminal Division of the Justice Department for the investigation of any criminal liability." The matter, Kennedy emphatically noted, "did not come before [his brother] on a preexisting conflict of interest" (S 34575). Applying Robert Kennedy's words to the matter of a supposed conflict is then a misapplication. Then, he and Dole and Hruska get into a tussle over Bayh's rather minor charge that Haynsworth had (technically) violated federal law as an officer of Carolina Vend-A-Matic by not filing required pension plan reports with the Department of Labor.

Once Bayh extracted himself from a debate that was clearly centering on a minor point, he introduced new voices into the debate: members of five Christian social action groups and law students at fifteen schools from all over the nation. All of these voices rejected Haynsworth because of both his ethical lapses and his record. The Student Bar Association Board at UCLA noted that, "Judge Haynsworth's insensitivity to judicial ethics has cast grave doubt on the propriety of appointing him to the Court whose support must ultimately rest in the respect accorded to it by the people" (S 34587). The United Students for Society's Rights at the University of Virginia Law School observed that, "Mr. Haynesworth's [sic] record as a federal judge is replete with unanimous reversals by the Supreme Court demonstrating his insensitivity to the directions of judicial thought, and to the important forces of change in our times, especially in the areas of labor and civil rights" (S 34587). On the other side of the question, Senator Dominick defended the nominee against these charges, and Colorado Senators Peter Dominick and Gordon Allott "did a colloquy" in defense. Then, after Senators Sparkman and Frank Moss (of Utah) spoke briefly, Dole introduced new inter-voices by quoting newspaper editorials endorsing Haynsworth from six newspapers from all corners (for example, Seattle, WA; Manchester, NH; Orlando, FL; and Dallas, TX) of the United States. Then, heavily quoting himself, Arizona Senator Paul Fannin defended Haynsworth against Bayh's charges.

Fannin also perhaps brought another matter into focus. He spoke about his and other Senators' opposition to Lyndon Johnson's nomination of Associate Justice Abe Fortas to be Chief Justice. The debate over Fortas joined the debate over Parker and the debate over Brandeis as the most often discussed previous confirmation debates. Parker and Brandeis functioned in the Haynsworth debate as reminders of the good men who can be lost if the Senate is swayed too much by attacks bordering on character assassination. Haynsworth's defenders wanted the Senate to avoid making the mistake that was almost made in the case of Brandeis and was made in the case of Parker. Fortas' story functioned differently in the debate and may be at the core of another argument operating in the debate but not fully voiced. Fortas was strongly opposed by the very legislators who were now most strongly supporting Haynsworth. As Fannin noted, "I examined Mr. Justice Fortas' judicial philosophy. I did not like what I found; I opposed him." As Fannin further observed, "I examined Judge Haynsworth's judicial philosophy. I like what I find; I support him" (S 34606). Because of these Senators' opposition—based on Fortas' liberal judicial philosophy, Fortas asked President Johnson to withdraw the nomination. Now, in the minds of liberal Senators opposed to Haynsworth, it may be payback time. The unvoiced opposition to Nixon's "plan" to make the Supreme Court more conservative coalesces nicely with this unvoiced call for revenge on the part of the liberals against the conservatives.

After Fannin spoke, Senator Jack Miller of Iowa gave the day's last address. He commented on what he found distasteful in the behavior of those who were opposing Haynsworth. He remarked that, "one of the things that has made it so difficult for me to oppose the nomination of Judge Haynsworth has been the proclivity for some of the opponents, aided and abetted by a few columnists and reporters, to raise false issues and innuendoes against the nominee." They were, he declared, "unbecoming the Senate" (S 34607). His comment perhaps pointed to one of several qualities that, as we shall shortly see, were lacking in the presentation being made by those opposed to Haynsworth.

As Vatz and Windt note, this debate and the Carswell debate that followed were rare insofar as the outcome was genuinely uncertain. Neither side was clearly the majority or the minority on the question before the Senate. Nonetheless, one can argue that—emotionally—those opposed to Haynsworth were the disempowered group. They—at least the Democrats dominant in the group—had just lost the White House in a bitter and close election. A few months before that, they had endured the wrenching experience of the disastrous 1968 Democratic National Convention in Chicago characterized by demonstrations, televised police brutality, and anticlimactic speeches by the annointed leaders, Humphrey and Muskie.

Given this disempowered position, the campaign to reject Haynsworth could have served as a carnivalesque moment for those—or some of those—opposing the nominee. It did not, however. Why? For one thing, there were, as Senator Miller noted, too many innuendoes and unfounded accusations being kicked about—for example, that Haynsworth was a business associate of Bobby Baker and that the nominee had played fast-and-loose with IRS regulations in donating a house to Furman University. Also, there was Senator Bayh's (or his staff's) sloppiness. In a hurry to indict Nixon's nominee, Bayh made several totally unfounded ethical charges. For example, Bayh charged that, "The judge had a conflict of interest when he participated in a 1961 case involving Kent Manufacturing Company," a subsidiary of which, Bayh incorrectly alleged, did business with Carolina Vend-A-Matic. And, Bayh charged that, "The judge had a conflict of interest in 1958 when he participated in a court case involving Olin Mathieson Chemical Company," whose parent company, Bayh incorrectly alleged, was Monsanto in which the judge owned stock (S 35123). Bayh had to retreat from these and other charges on several occasions during the debate, referring to his previous letters and statements of apology. He seemed reckless, defensive. And there was the division among the opponents (who were drawn from both paries)—some of whom wanted to argue about ethics, others about school desegregation, others about labor relations. There was even division on the question of whether it was appropriate for the Senate to consider a nominee's stand on issues or judicial philosophy when that body offered its advice and, presumably, its consent. Not surprisingly then, halfway through the debate, the opposition seemed disunified and tired, not enlivened by carnivalesque energy.

DAY FOUR

Senator John Williams of Delaware, who began the debate on November 19, is one of the Haynsworth opponents who believed judicial philosophy should be irrelevant:

> In my opinion agreement or disagreement with the man's political philosophy is no valid basis for opposition to his confirmation. In fact, if this argument were to be accepted as the basis for a decision I personally would have enthusiastically endorsed the confirmation of Judge Haynsworth when his nomination was first announced, and by the same token I would have voted against many of the preceding Justices appointed by former administrations. Under our Constitution nominations to fill vacancies on the Supreme Court are made by the President, and it is to be expected that in making this selection the President will nominate men whose social or political philosophy more nearly coincides with his own. Had Mr. Humphrey been elected President I am sure he would have named a liberal to fill this vacancy, and the country expects Mr. Nixon to name a man of more conservative background. (S 34825)

Therefore, Williams premised his rejection of the nominee on the ethical questions. He quoted Haynsworth heavily because he was interested in pointing out disturbing contradictions among the statements the nominee had made. Senators John Tower of Texas, Carl Curtis of Nebraska, and J.

Caleb Boggs of Delaware, who spoke next, also focused on the ethical questions, with Curtis especially concerned about the accusation involving the gift of a house to Furman. We hear the usual inter-voices, and Curtis used numerous examples of prosopopoeia, such as the words the Senate had *not* heard:

> I repeat, Mr. President, that to my knowledge not a single Senator has risen on this floor and said, "Here is a transaction in which Judge Haynsworth was dishonest." Not a single Senator has risen in this place, to my knowledge, and said, "Here is a case in which Judge Haynsworth enriched himself by reason of a matter being litigated before him," or, "Here is a case in which the decision was influenced by financial considerations." (S 34844–45)

Arizona Senator Barry Goldwater introduced a somewhat different voice—his own, personally relating what it felt like to be the target of character assassination during the 1964 presidential campaign:

> I doubt if it is necessary to remind this Senate that in 1964 I was pictured by my critics in the public media of this Nation as a man totally ruthless and almost completely devoid of any humanitarian feelings. In a few short months of campaigning, I became—judging from the appearances of me which sprung up in the public print and on television—a candidate who was determined to abolish the American social security system and start World War III by the indiscriminate use of nuclear weapons. . . . It can become dangerously close to the abhorrent practice which all Americans deplore—the practice of character assassination. (S 34948)

His personal story was a refreshing change from the quoted words of scholars and lawyers that had thus far dominated the debate. Senator Stennis, the next lengthy speaker, will also tell a personal story—how the workload and work habits of a trial judge can result in his not realizing that he has a technical conflict of interest:

> We do not like to use ourselves as illustrations. However, I had the responsibility, for almost 10 years, of being a trial judge in a court of unlimited jurisdiction, involving civil and criminal cases. . . . I have held 3 or 4 weeks of court and have been almost overwhelmed by the great number of cases that involved the signing of decrees, including those

which would take a man's house away from him, or would sentence him to the penitentiary or sometimes sentence him to the loss of his life. That is not pleasant. . . . What does a judge do? He passes on the easy ones first and forgets them. He works hard and worries over and over again about the hard cases. I do not have any doubt that that was what happened in Judge Haynsworth's case. The *Brunswick* case was easy; it involved a conflict of liens. The court decided that it was an easy case. Another judge wrote the opinion, and the case passed out of Judge Haynsworth's mind. Just as he said, he overlooked it. (S 34852)

Stennis' inter-voices were interesting in two other respects. First, he repeated newspaper editorials and columns critical of Haynsworth that were published immediately after his nomination in the *New York Times*, the *Washington Post*, and the *Los Angeles Times*. The speed with which these denunciations appeared did indeed suggest that the opposition was not entirely against Judge Haynsworth but, rather, Nixon and/or what Nixon was attempting to accomplish. Second, he cited and quoted Nixon far more than any other Senator. He seemed thereby to frame the debate more in terms of the Nixon administration's story than in terms of Clement Haynsworth's.

Another Southern Senator, Spessard Holland of Florida, referred to the "hundreds, if not thousands, of letters" (S 34853) he had received supporting Haynsworth. He also, like Dole earlier, referred to and quoted editorials endorsing the nominee. Since one editorial implied that Bayh was acting as the agent of organized labor, Bayh and Holland got into a verbal scuffle at this point. Senator Allott took over and, virtually ignoring Holland's remarks, praised and repeated Stennis.

Senator George Murphy of California spoke on Haynsworth's behalf. He focused on the labor relations issues, not the ethical ones. The voices he introduced were by now quite familiar. He did, however, add to the storytelling that Goldwater began and Stennis continued by narrating an account of the character assassination experienced by Richard Nixon in the mid-1950s:

As I said a few days ago in this Chamber, I recall an instance when an attempt was made to destroy by character assassination a man who is a good friend of mine. There was a rumor, then it was published, then it was recited, and then it was spread across the country like wildfire, that he had done something wrong. It was an attempt to destroy his political life. Then in preparation was a second rumor—that he had an inordinate amount of furniture in his house. Where did he get the money

to buy it? Nobody said he had done anything wrong. But they posed
the question, and the question took on all the characteristics of an assault, of accusation. Where did he get it? The fact of the matter is that
he did not have it. There was no truth. It was, once again, the appearance of impropriety, started by a rumor, a dishonest, evil rumor, without any basis or foundation. Then there was a third attempt. . . . Three
attempts were made to create the appearance of impropriety. The man
against whom this was designed is now the President of the United
States. (S 34858)

The last lengthy speech was by Hawaii Senator Hiram Fong. He supported his arguments with the usual voices. Noteworthy was his decision, as
Day Four of the debate closed, to equally address the school desegregation,
labor relations, and ethical questions. No one issue seemed truly in the foreground by itself.

DAY FIVE

By now, all arguments, both on the surface and beneath the surface, have
been discussed—except perhaps the trickiest. As the roster of Senators on
Haynsworth's side suggests, he was seen by many not just as a conservative
nominee, but as a Southern nominee. Thus, attacks on him, especially if
civil rights or labor relations were brought in, could be construed as attacks
on "The South." No such anti-Southern argument was explicitly voiced by
those challenging Haynsworth's appointment; nonetheless, the argument is
entailed by the utterances opponents are offering and is therefore functioning in the debate, prompting some displays of solidarity on the part of
Southern Senators against this anti-South position. Much as the unvoiced
argument against "The South" functioned as double-voiced discourse in the
poll tax debate analyzed in Chapter Six, that same argument functioned
here. And, much as the Southerners exhibited carnivalesque energy in the
1960 debate as they defended their home states, the Southerners here displayed at least some inklings of that energy.

Two such Southerners began the debating on Day Five, November 20.
Arkansas' John McClellan focused on the ethical question. He brought up
the Fortas matter but with a different twist. He argued that those who excused actions by Fortas that had the appearance of impropriety are the very
ones now impugning Haynsworth. He suggested that the difference was that
Haynsworth was a Southerner:

Since the day he was nominated, Clement Haynsworth has been subjected to intense criticism. No sooner was the name announced than he was being characterized as antilabor, a segregationist, and far too conservative. That, Mr. President, has been claimed by the same people who have heretofore contended that one should not consider the philosophy of a nominee, that the only thing one should consider is whether he is professionally qualified and of good character. Now the situation is reversed and they say, "We have to take into account the philosophy in this instance; it would not do to overlook it." So we see that it depends on the nominee, and sometimes I think the section of the country from which the nominee comes, as to whether philosophy is important or whether it should be disregarded. (S 35120)

Senator Sam Ervin also highlighted Fortas' ethical problems. He tried also to bring to the debate the voices of average Americans by quoting many letters he had received—for example, letters from North Carolina teachers objecting to the position on Haynsworth that the National Education Association had taken. For example, he quoted one Wallace I. West, who told the president of the National Education Association (N.E.A.) that, "The statement issued by you criticizing President Nixon for proposing the name of Judge Clement Haynsworth to the Supreme Court and requesting him to withdraw the nomination was totally uncalled for. I am a member of the N.E.A. and you certainly do not speak for me and I am sure you do not speak for thousands of other N.E.A. members" (S 35125).

In general, the supporters of Haynsworth—many of whom are very conservative—are both the storytellers and the users of the voices of average Americans in this debate. Curiously, they are using the inter-voices heavily relied upon by the women of the Senate in the first three debates examined in this study. The implication then may be drawn that the use of these particular inter-voices is not gendered or that those who speak on behalf of "the other"—be it women and minorities or "the silent majority"—tend to introduce citizens' voices and personal anecdotes. Alterity rather than gender per se may be the crucial factor.

Allott followed Ervin's lead. He focused on the labor relations issue, not the ethical matters. He introduced into the debate the voices of the union rank-and-file, who objected to the Warren Court and, therefore, supported Haynsworth's appointment. Allott refers to them as "the silent majority" (S 35128), stylizing President Nixon and thereby adding Nixon's authority to the argument about where the American people really stood.

Alaska Senator Ted Stevens then spoke in support of Haynsworth. He avoided citing or quoting any of the voluminous evidence being used in the debate. Instead, he referred to his colleagues and to Eisenhower, Nixon, and officials in Nixon's Department of Justice, all of whom had, at one time or another, endorsed Haynsworth. New Jersey Senator Clifford Case, opposed to Haynsworth, was equally spare in the inter-voices he used, quoting the late Senator George Norris, referring to Javits' presentation on Haynsworth's civil rights record, and quoting Haynsworth's 1963 decision concerning the closing of public schools in Prince Edward County, Virginia, in order to avoid integration, and the Supreme Court's 1964 reversal of it. Referring to Haynsworth's decision, Case said:

At best his statement indicates a degree of insensitivity to human rights unfitting the tribunal to which the American people look as the ultimate protector of constitutional guarantees. . . . I believe there can be no doubt that Judge Haynsworth's confirmation by the Senate would be taken by great numbers of our people as the elevation of a symbol of resistance to the historical movement toward equal justice for every American citizen. This appointment, at this time, would drive more deeply the wedge between the black community and the other minorities on the one hand and, on the other, the rest of American society. (S 35131)

After Case entertained challenges from Cook and Allott, Javits took the floor. After stating what his position was on whether Senators should or should not consider a nominee's judicial philosophy, he reestablished his position on Haynsworth's civil rights record by focusing on what he saw to be the several crucial court cases. Wyoming Senator Gale McGee reinforced Javits' position by entering Princeton University Professor Gary Orfield's testimony before the Judiciary Committee into the *Record*; Senator Metcalf reinforced Bayh's position by using a curious example of prosopopoeia: what former NFL Commissioner Pete Rozelle might have said to Joe Namath about the appearance of impropriety in the Jets quarterback's being part-owner of the Bachelors III nightclub in New York City (S 35137).

At this point in the debate, we see a combination of a few voices, a few new arguments, and a great deal of rebuttal. Among the more interesting presentations—for various reasons—during the remainder of the fifth day were Dole's discussion of the nominee's conservative decisions on pornography and Maryland Senator Charles Matthias' restrained and well-reasoned discussion of Haynsworth's ethical lapses. The former was interesting because it introduced a new issue; the latter because it was well done.

On this fifth day of debate, several of the speakers began taking turns entering into the record documents that they believed were crucial in the debate: Spong introduced Professor Charles Allan Wright; Hollings, Professor William VanAlstyne; Hruska, a Cheyenne *State Tribune* editorial; Bayh, the unnamed dean of the Yale Law School and UCLA law professor David Mellinkoff. Should a Senator have chosen to read the record, then he or she would have heard the many voices these inserts included; but, should a Senator not have had the time or the inclination, then all that was heard was a thud of many pages being added to an already long debate.

Although the civil rights charges were being focused on for a large part of the day, the day's debating ended with Bayh attempting to sustain his unethical behavior charges against increasingly hostile and heated responses by Hruska and Hollings, the latter heavily—and at times sarcastically—attacking Bayh:

The Senator from Indiana . . . could not wait for the Judiciary Committee to file its report. He said this debate is an important thing and we ought to carry it on the floor and we ought not to carry it on in the committee. He did not wait for his own committee's report, the majority report, and he could not wait to get in his own minority views; but in the news, in the headlines, on the TV screen, we saw the bill of particulars charging crimes, 37 violations of the canons, and at least four violations of the statute. (S 35174)

Get that headline tomorrow. Can you see that in the *Washington Post*? "Senator Bayh Says Do Not Believe Judge Haynsworth Was Feathering Own Nest." Would that not be grand. You could really sell some copies of that paper down in South Carolina. (S 35176)

The most noteworthy address, however, of the last hours of the fifth day was that of Senator Eastland. First, his speech was interesting because he very explicitly interpreted the attack on Haynsworth as an attack on "The South." He referred to an article entitled "Does Supreme Court Need a Southern Accent," which suggested that Nixon chose Haynsworth because he was a Southerner and, furthermore, that Haynsworth was a problematic choice because he was a Southerner. Eastland then said:

I do not know whether this columnist has more courage or less sense than her associates, but at least this writer was perceptive enough to recognize this underlying motive behind the Haynsworth opposition and to lay it squarely on the line. At least this writer has said what others are embarrassingly reluctant to admit, but extremely anxious to exploit. Witness after witness has pointed up the nominee's Southern background. They have repeatedly, with bitter tone and inflection of voice, referred to the Judge as a "fifth generation South Carolinian." They have emphasized his Southern background in order to exploit the prejudices and resentments that still linger in the minds of some Americans toward the people of that region. (S 35151)

Eastland furthermore argued that the resentment, rooted in the past, was being exacerbated by an ongoing economic conflict. He noted that, "The repeated references to the loss of Northern industry to the South ran like a broken record throughout the hearings" (S 35151). Eastland tried to remove the veil from the "the sectional animosity" (S 35151) that he believed was behind much of the opposition to Haynsworth. Second, in addition to bringing the anti-South argument into the open, Eastland also shed light on two other somewhat hidden arguments. Eastland noted that, "there are those who justify their conduct in this matter by saying, We are only giving Haynsworth the same treatment Fortas got" (S 35153), thereby bringing the revenge argument into the light. Eastland referred to "the paranoid psychology that compels the liberal establishment to try to silence every voice that is raised against them and to destroy every man who cannot be counted on 100 percent" (S 35153), thereby bringing the liberals vs. Nixon drama into the light.

The third reason Eastland's address was noteworthy was that he brings the voice of the late President John F. Kennedy heavily into the debate. Kennedy's voice, one would suspect, would probably have been on the side of those opposing Haynsworth if Kennedy had been alive. Eastland's use of Kennedy's voice was therefore a striking move. He used Kennedy to two ends. First, he referred to Kennedy's portrait of Senator Lucius Q. Lamar of Mississippi in *Profiles in Courage*. He thereby linked Senator Lamar and Senators in 1969 as politicians who must decide, as Lamar did, between principle and political expediency when casting crucial votes. The "glow" Kennedy provided Lamar, who did not vote for the Bland Silver Act, is available—Eastland suggested—for those who choose principle and vote for Haynsworth. Second, he referred to Kennedy's famous 1960 speech to the Houston Ministerial Association in which he asked the gathered Southern ministers not to judge him as a Catholic but as an American statesman. Eastland's point was that, in Kennedy's spirit, the Senators in 1969 should not judge Haynsworth as a Southerner but as an American jurist. Eastland quoted Kennedy's words. Then, in a brilliant example of stylization and prosopopoeia, Eastland offered Haynsworth's imagined paraphrase of Kennedy:

> If I should lose on the real issues, I shall return to my seat as chief judge of the Fourth Circuit Court of Appeals, satisfied that I have tried my best and was fairly judged. But if this nomination is decided on the basis that every American from the South has lost his chance to serve on the Supreme Court, then it is the whole Nation that will be the loser. (S 35151)

DAY SIX

Day Six, November 21, 1969, was, with the exception of one speech, rather anticlimactic. It began with brief remarks. Then, South Dakota Senator Karl Mundt spoke. The inter-voices he used are very heavily those of his Senate colleagues, creating an echo effect. He also added Charles Evans Hughes' name to the roster of previously debated nominees. Hughes joined Fortas, Parker, Brandeis, and others in a list that suggested that, in many ways, this debate did not begin with Nixon's nomination of Clement Haynsworth. Javits then sustained the echo effect by referring heavily to colleagues' previous statements.

Following a detour taken by Senator H. A. Williams of New Jersey to discuss whether or not the nominee had violated the Securities and Exchange Act, Thurmond offered a lengthy address. This is the noteworthy speech. He discussed the labor relations and ethical issues, curiously ignoring the school desegregation matter, and then tried to bring the voices of the American voters into the debate. He referred to the verdict voters reached in 1968; he stylized Nixon by referring to many who voted for Nixon as "the silent majority":

> Mr. President, there are millions of Americans who are watching silently while we debate—watching silently but not deafly nor blindly. They warned us in 1968 that a vast majority of the people in this country were tired of the so-called "liberalism." They said it at the ballot box, and they said it loudly and clearly, although wordlessly. Mr. President, we must heed that message. There is a mob in the streets, a mass

of mindless, screaming militants. We have a choice, and that choice is here now before us today. We can listen to the silent majority, or we can listen to those who would have us abide by the rule of force—the rule of force that dictates that he who screams the loudest is right. (S 35380)

Thurmond then proceeded to quote some of the silent majority's voices—twenty-eight letters and fifteen articles—all favorable to Haynsworth. At least one article, entitled "The Liberals' Revenge," suggested that those opposed to Haynsworth were enacting revenge for Fortas' defeat:

> While liberals conducted a campaign of what Vice President Agnew called "character assassination" against Judge Clement Haynsworth, Howard K. Smith reported in gleeful tones on his ABC television broadcast that conservatives of the country were about to get their comeuppance. Blaming conservatives for the uproar that brought about the resignation of Justice Abe Fortas, President Johnson's choice for Chief Justice, Smith said that Fortas had done nothing wrong. He said that Fortas, by advising the President on Executive matters, had merely given the appearance of impropriety. And now the conservatives' attacks on Fortas on that basis had come back to haunt them, with liberals using the same type of ammunition to defeat the appointment of Judge Haynsworth to the vacancy on the U.S. Supreme Court. (S 35384)

Another article, this one from the *Charleston News and Courier*, noted that, "Members of a minority still discriminated against in government are Southerners. They are often treated as outcasts." The article declared that, "It is shocking and tragic that at this point in American history sectional prejudice is directed against the South, and that a man of demonstrated ability [Haynsworth] should be opposed because he hails from a Southern state" (S 35385). The largely unvoiced double-voiced discourse of the debate was surfacing late in the words of the citizens, editorialists, and conservative columnists Strom Thurmond quoted.

Shortly after Thurmond concluded, Bayh and Hruska summarized for the opposed sides. Bayh, not surprisingly, emphasized the ethical matters. Hruska followed suit but also recalled the many general recommendations and endorsements Haynsworth had received. Then, the Senate voted 55–45 to reject Nixon's nominee.

The vote did not end the debating on the 21st. Several, especially on the losing side, wanted to comment on the vote. The vote also did not end either the voiced or the unvoiced arguments against Haynsworth, for Nixon, several months later, would send to the Senate the nomination of another Southern conservative with a questionable past with regards to race relations. As Vatz and Windt suggest by treating the debate over Harold G. Carswell as if it were but an extension of that over Haynsworth, the debate in late November 1969 lacked finalizability. And, as several speakers suggested during the Haynsworth debate, it lacked a definitive beginning as well, for the debates over Brandeis, Parker, Fortas, and others foregrounded the consideration of Nixon's nominee. The two issues of prejudice (be it sectional or religious) and judicial philosophy intertwined with partisan politics in the Haynsworth case as well as these previous ones. These matters—at least some of them—play a role even today when a Supreme Court vacancy occurs. Each new debate represents a continuation of a dialogue—sometimes cordial, sometimes not—that began long before Richard M. Nixon uttered the name Clement Haynsworth.

Chapter Eight

The House of Representatives Impeaches William Jefferson Clinton

The previous five chapters have dealt with debates that occurred in the U.S. Senate. In general, debates on the Senate side of "The Hill" are more compelling because the actors involved are all better known. There are only fifty, and many of them have achieved a measure of national stature because of either their longevity in the Senate or their candidacy for the presidency. Debates in the House of Representatives are also interesting, and, as this chapter will demonstrate, they can be studied using the Bakhtinian paradigm outlined in Chapter Two just as readily as can Senate debates.

As we move from Senate to House, a few communication-related differences do, however, need to be discussed briefly. Although no one has systematically contrasted Senate and House, several differences are apparent in conversations with House members and when viewing or reading the House floor debates. First, the level of formality and ritualistic courtesy is lower in the House than in the Senate. Media commentators often make an issue of this difference when a member of the House seeks a seat in the Senate. Will he or she be able to make the transition in style from the rough-and-tumble of the House to the deference born of six-year terms characteristic of the Senate? Thomas Kane, in a special issue of *Argumentation and Advocacy* that he edited, explains Pennsylvania Senator Rick Santorum's initial communication difficulties in the Senate in terms of the difficulty of this transition, especially if one is blinded to the existence of political customs by ideology. Second, the level of speech preparation is generally lower in the House than in the Senate. This difference is the result of House members having smaller staffs and lower budgets. (This difference seems to be diminishing.) Third, the tendency to avail oneself of the opportunity to revise and extend one's floor remarks is higher in the House than in the Senate. This difference may be the consequence of smaller House staffs: work that would be done prior to an address in the Senate often must be accomplished after the address per se in the House. In addition, as Kathleen Hall Jamieson noted in her Carroll C. Arnold lecture delivered at the National Communication Association convention in November 1999, revising may well be a Representative's way of covering up incivility.

This third difference raises a textual problem for one who wishes to study debates on the floor of the House of Representatives. The textual problem has been studied by communication scholars periodically. In 1942, Zon Robinson and Elizabeth McPherson published separate articles on the subject in the *Quarterly Journal of Speech*; then, in the early 1960s, Earl Cain, Wallace W. Stevens, and J. A. Hendrix published separate essays—Stevens' in *Communication Studies*; Cain's and Hendrix's in the *Southern Speech Journal*. In 1977, David F. Quadro offered an update in a *Western Journal of Communication* article. The consensus of these studies is that, although there are differences between what occurs on the floor and what sees print in the *Congressional Record*, the differences ought not to impede critical analysis. There are, these studies note, rare cases, especially in the House, where the revisions and the extensions are so numerous that the debate on the floor and the debate in print are very different. Such is the case for the debate over articles of impeachment offered by the House Judiciary Committee to the full House on December 18 and 19th, 1998. Fortunately, recently, the editors of the *Record* have made a distinction among what was actually said, extensions that fit the flow of the debate, and extensions that are truly postscripts. They have printed the postscripts at the end of a given day's record, and they have used a different font to distinguish in the text between what was said (albeit edited) and the closely-related added remarks. These editorial decisions allow the critic to choose what he or she analyses.

The critic's decision may well vary from case to case, depending on the research question in mind. In the case of the impeachment debate, I wanted to examine the polyphony of the two-day event. Thus, I excluded both types of extensions from my examination. But, as Bakhtin notes, discourse does not have neat temporal boundaries. Thus, these extensions do indeed become part of an ongoing debate. If one were to broaden one's perspective and include the voices in these extensions, one would not, however, find much to contradict an analysis based just on what was actually spoken. In this case, the extensions amplified, not altered.

This particular House debate features far more extending of remarks than is normally the case. The proliferation is the result of the time limitation leaders in the House agreed to so as not to signal that legislative body's obsession with either exposing Clinton's sexual behavior or attacking the president. Within the agreed-to limited amount of time, leaders wanted to give every member a chance to speak. Thus, the speeches became briefer and briefer as the managers for the two sides allotted less and less time to succeeding House members. The debate then reads more like a string of very short addresses, in which member after member presents her or his rationale for voting "Yea" or "Nay" on the proposed articles of impeachment.

VOICES

Michigan Representative John Conyers at one point on Friday the 18th rejected the very idea of the debate resolving the issues before the House (H 11808). In Conyers' mind, the debate was but a show. On the other hand, Wisconsin Congressman F. James Sensenbrenner characterized the debate as "one of the finest debates that the House of Representatives has had" (H 12034). He seemed to believe that the two-day event was far more than just a show.

The truth of the matter seems to lie somewhere between Conyers' and Sensenbrenner's assessments. The shapelessness of the debate—members of the House Judiciary Committee followed by random others—was reasonably typical, for almost all Congressional debating features a degree of random speaking. Even the attempt to derail the motion by amendment—in this case, a "sense of the House" resolution that would have, in effect, censured the president—was typical. But, despite this relative formlessness, several issues were indeed discussed. The appropriateness of censuring Clinton rather than impeaching him was addressed by both impeachment advocates and opponents. They looked at historical precedents and constitutional law closely. The proper use of the House's impeachment power was also addressed by both sides, complete with many references to the "Founding Fathers'" legislative intent. And, at least the speakers in favor of impeachment looked closely at what they argued were Clinton's perjury and obstruction of justice. Those opposed to impeachment occasionally impugned the evidence or questioned the Republicans' and/or Special Prosecutor Kenneth Starr's motives. There was clash, even though Clinton's defenders only rarely played the role of defense attorney and argued that the president was guiltless.

The debate also developed an energy—perhaps a carnivalesque one—as it proceeded throughout Friday. Both sides were showing increased camaraderie; the noise level—both of anger and restrained joviality—was up, on the floor and in the gallery. What eventually stopped the flow of energy was

Louisiana Representative Bob Livingston's announcement in his floor address on the morning of the 19th that he would not seek election to the position of Speaker of the House. He announced that, "I will not stand for Speaker of the House on January 6, but rather I shall remain as a backbencher in this Congress that I so dearly love for approximately 6 months into the 106th Congress, whereupon I shall vacate my seat and ask my Governor to call a special election to take my place" (H 11970). He was resigning because of the exposure of his adulterous behavior by *Hustler* magazine publisher Larry Flynt; furthermore, he was challenging President Clinton to do the same.

The next few speakers, already in line with their brief remarks in hand, proceeded as if nothing dramatic had happened. In fact, the very next speaker, Representative Jose Serrano of New York proceeded to attack "[t]he Republican right wing" (H 11970). Eventually, however, Livingston's action sobered the Congress. Perhaps the speech that drained any potential carnivalesque energy from the debate was Texas Representative Tom DeLay's. He began by saying, "I do not know if I can make this speech." Then, he commented on the morning's events:

> There is no greater American in my mind, at least today, than the gentleman from Louisiana because he understood what this debate was all about. It was about honor and decency and integrity and the truth, everything we honor in this country. (H 11974)

DeLay quickly politicized the moment, praising outgoing Speaker of the House Newt Gingrich and Livingston; implicitly criticizing Clinton. No matter; his emotional address ended the partisan frivolity. The next several speakers all talked in depressed tones. And, picking up very little of Friday's verve, the debate limped forward to the ultimate votes.

Throughout the debate those in favor of impeachment spoke differently than those against. Those in favor adopted a tone their critics termed "pious"; those against a tone of outrage. This difference is striking; so is the difference between the male speakers and the female speakers, regardless of side. There were, it would seem, "party lines" in the debate. Republicans argued that the accusations against Clinton had nothing to do with sex; rather they had to do with perjury and obstruction of justice. Democrats argued either that Clinton's behavior was wrong but not grounds for impeachment, and/or they denounced those in and out of Congress who were so intent upon "getting" Clinton that they would not even permit the House to vote on censure. If one examines the speeches delivered by women, they followed these scripts. These speeches were also succinct. The pro-impeachment addresses (Mary Bono of California, Nancy Johnson of Connecticut, Sue Myrick of North Carolina, Ileana Ros-Lehtinen of Florida, Heather Wilson of New Mexico, Helen Chenoweth of Idaho, Marge Roukema of New Jersey, and Tillie Fowler of Florida) were virtually carbon copies of each other. The anti-impeachment addresses (too many to list) varied only insofar as some denounced certain factions within the G.O.P. with more flagrant language than others. Diana Degette of Colorado, Donna Christian-Green of the Virgin Islands, Louise Slaughter of New York, Lynn Woolsey of California, Carolyn Maloney of New York, Loretta Sanchez of California, and others characterized the G.O.P. as partisan and unfair. At the other extreme, Rosa DeLauro of Connecticut accused the opposition Republicans of "naked partisanship," Maxine Waters of California accused them of "unbridled hatred," Carrie Meeks of Florida characterized them as "gonad shriveling," and Barbara Lee of California characterized them as "authoritarian" and "dangerous." The men, on the other hand, did not follow the scripts. They spoke at greater length, and they were more likely to pursue detours. The extensions they submitted to the *Record* were also typically longer. This verbosity is noticeable at both the beginning and the end of the two-day event, so it was not just the higher ranking committee members on both sides who were "out-speaking" the women. One can perhaps see in this gender difference both the effect of socialization upon young females to follow rules and the inclination of those gendered female to work as members of a group.

A Bakhtinian perspective attunes the critic to the polyphony of a debate—to the many voices. Thus, a critic must resist grouping speakers together too quickly, for that grouping will obscure what the individual speakers say and how. Nonetheless, sometimes people do speak as members of a group. In Congress, many legislators do, at times, speak as party members. What my foregoing analysis of the women who spoke during the impeachment debate suggests is that, in this debate, they spoke primarily as such. In other debates—for example, that over Admiral Kelso's retirement rank discussed in Chapter Four, gender will take priority over party.

In the impeachment debate, there is, however, one group that does stand out as offering a different set of arguments in a somewhat different way. This is the group of African Americans. Their style is more flamboyant, and they see the attack on President Clinton as an attack on Black America.

Consider Maxine Waters of California. She associated the following adjectives with those who are pushing for impeachment: "partisan," "extremist," "radical," "despicable"; and she attributes to them "raw, unmasked, unbridled hatred and meanness." Why do they so hate Clinton? According to Waters, "the President is guilty of being a populist leader who opened up government and access to the poor, to minorities, to women, and to the working class." Clinton is not "owned by the good ole southern boys or the good ole eastern establishment" (H 11797–98).

Consider Danny Davis of Illinois. He referred to the impeachment process comically as "the nightmare before Christmas" and with-an-edge as "this lynching in the people's House." He stated that the debate "is not about impeaching Bill Clinton." Rather, the debate is "about impeaching affirmative action, impeaching women's rights" (H 11853).

Consider Carrie Meeks of Florida. She repeatedly characterized the pro-impeachment forces as "partisan," and, somewhat comically, termed the process "gonadal agony" and "gonad shriveling." She also contextualized the interpreting of the Constitution that was occurring in the House on December 18th and 19th by noting that more than a century earlier many had interpreted the Constitution in such a way that her forbears were not only denied suffrage but declared property.

Finally, consider Jesse Jackson, Jr., of Illinois. Like Waters, Davis, and Meeks, he accused the Republicans of "impeaching affirmative action" and other social programs important to the economic development of African Americans. He, like Meeks, contextualized the impeachment debate by treating Bill Clinton's advocacy of such programs, strong African American support for the president, and the Republican assault on Clinton as but the latest installment in a struggle for economic and social justice that began with the Civil War.

INTER-VOICES

The brevity of most of the speeches delivered during the debate precluded extensive quoting and lengthy storytelling. Nonetheless, the speakers offered a rich array of inter-voices. References to authorities and brief quotations of them were quite numerous. It is interesting to classify these references and quotations into three categories: the "Founding Fathers"; testimony or evidence relevant to Clinton's particular actions; and the American voters. Speakers introduced the "voices" of all three, but there were some noteworthy differences in how these "voices" were used.

A critic with stronger social scientific inclinations than myself could find many items to count and compare if pursuing a Bakhtinian analysis. I did just a bit of counting myself in this instance. First, I wanted to see if there were differences between the pro-impeachment and the anti-impeachment speakers in their relative use of the "Founding Fathers" and voters' voices. I found that those opposed to impeachment used both kinds about equally. However, those in favor of impeachment cited the "Founding Fathers" twice as often as they did the American voting public. Second, I wanted to see if there were differences among males favoring impeachment, females favoring impeachment, males opposed, and females opposed in their relative use of legal supporting material (defined as both references to the "Founding Fathers" and evidence relevant to Clinton's conduct) as opposed to the voting public's voices. Females cited both kinds of voices about equally; males opposed to impeachment cited legal voices slightly more than constituent voices; and males in favor of impeachment cited legal voices almost nine times more than those of voters. Male use of inter-voices then was more legalistic than the female, with the discourse of males favoring impeachment being extremely legalistic. Put another way, all speakers but males who favored impeachment seemed to be trying, through the voices they cited or quoted, to balance the views of voting citizens against more traditionally authoritative voices. The pro-impeachment males relied on traditional authority, the public (almost) be damned.

Whenever an authority—traditional or that vested in the people—is cited or quoted, that authority's voice is "heard" in support of whatever position the speaker is taking. When competing speakers want a voice to be "heard" on their behalf, they may engage in a battle for the particular authority. Such battles occurred throughout the impeachment debate. The "Founding Fathers," for example, were cited or quoted often. To the extent there were two sides in the debate, both sides voiced Jefferson, Hamilton, Washington, Adams, Jay, Marshall, and others frequently. The result in this debate was that these historic voices ended up speaking for no rhetor or no side in particular. They provided something of an historical chorus.

Similar battles were fought over the Bible, Jerry Ford, Bob Dole, Barbara Jordan, and Abraham Lincoln. Consider the following collection of references to the Bible:

RICHARD GEPHART of Missouri (opposed): In the Book of Isaiah in the Bible, it was said, "Judgment is turned away backward and justice stands far off." (H 11778)

ROBERT MENDENDEZ of New Jersey (opposed): I warn my colleagues that they will reap the bitter harvest of the unfair partisan seeds they sow today. (H 11780)

JOHN LEWIS of Georgia (opposed): Let he that has no sin cast the first stone. Who among us has not sinned? (H 11782)

ALBERT WYNN of Maryland (opposed): Let he who is without sin cast the first stone. (H 11828)

DENNIS KUCINICH of Ohio (opposed): [B]ehold the prophetic power of the Biblical injunction "Judge not, that you not be judged." In the name of all the people who have suffered a dark night of assault, feel the might of the warning, let he who is without sin cast the first stone. (H 11844)

BART STUPAK of Michigan (opposed): Sister Margaret reminded me of the Biblical story of how the men who would stone a prostitute were the very men that paid her for her services, and how they were challenged by Jesus, who said, "Let he who is without sin cast the first stone." (H 11892)

DAVE WELDON of Florida (in favor): [S]everal people on the minority side have risen today and quoted the scripture, "Judge not, that you not be judged." Careful reading of this scripture makes it quite clear that the message is not that we should never judge or exercise judgment. (H 11897)

MARGE ROUKEMA of New Jersey (in favor): But this cup cannot pass us by. (H 11971)

ELIJAH CUMMINGS of Maryland (opposed): As David cried out to the Lord in the Book of Psalms—"For I know my transgressions, and my sin is ever before me. Against thee, and thee only, have I sinned, and done that which is evil in thy sight, so that thou art justified in thy sentence and blameless in thy judgment." (H 11971)

Two passages, one aptly dealing with one caught in adultery, were cited by those defending the president. Through these passages, Jesus spoke to those accusing Clinton. Representative Weldon of Florida tried to reinterpret one of the two passages in a manner more favorable to the pro-impeachment speakers. Representative Roukema of New Jersey took a different tack, ascribing Jesus' voice to those Representatives who must, even though it is agonizing, vote to impeach. Representative Cummings of Maryland simply attached Christ's precursor David's confession to Clinton's, thereby elevating the latter's public statement. Cummings' point was that Clinton had asked his family for forgiveness; and that ought to end the matter.

Just as speakers wanted Jesus' voice to sound through theirs, speakers wanted those of former Republican President Gerald Ford and defeated Republican presidential candidate Bob Dole. The following quotations—arranged in the order they were spoken in the debate—demonstrate how these voices could have helped the anti-impeachment cause. Further, the quotations reveal pro-impeachment Republicans trying to reclaim the voices of Ford and Dole:

VIC FAZIO of California (opposed): Jerry Ford, upon assuming the presidency after Watergate, said our long national nightmare is now over. (H 11798)

NITA LOFGREN of New York (opposed): The country is waiting for grownups to walk into this Chamber and stop this madness, but, alas, those Republicans with the maturity and judgment to ask that censure be utilized as an alternative, such as former President Ford and former Senator Dole, have been ignored by the majority in this House. (H 11800)

TOM LANTOS of California (opposed): The censure vote we are seeking is supported by our former Republican colleague, the former Republican President of the United States of America, Gerald Ford, who is renowned for his fairness. The censure vote we seek is supported by the former Republican leader of the United States Senate and the Republican candidate for President in 1996, Senator Bob Dole. (H 11808)

FRANK RIGGS of California (in favor): [I]n the last 48 hours I have spoken to both former President Ford and Bob Dole. Both men emphatically told me . . . that they would vote to impeach, that they felt it was the duty of the House . . . to vote for the articles of impeachment. (H 11808)

BOB GOODLATTE of Virginia (in favor): I ask that a letter received from Senator Bob Dole dated today be placed in the record. I will read a part of that: "It is entirely appropriate for the U.S. House of Representatives to debate and vote on articles of impeachment at this time." (H 11809)

BART STUPAK of Michigan (opposed): I agree that the President's behavior was inappropriate and immoral and that he must be held accountable, but, as Bob Dole wrote in the *New York Times*, a bipartisan resolution of censure would be a proper Congressional response. (H 11892)

JOHN SPRATT of South Carolina (opposed): I come down on the side of President Ford and Senator Dole. I think President Clinton should be censured, censured severely. (H 11903)

JERRY COSTELLO of Illinois (opposed): Mr. President, I agree with former President Gerald Ford and the former majority leader, Senator Bob Dole, that the Congress should censure the President of the United States. (H 11905)

DAVID MINGE of Minnesota (opposed): [M]y Republican friends, they have even refused to accept the advice of President Ford and Presidential candidate Dole that we proceed with a censure or rebuke alternative. (H 11920)

DEBBIE STABENOW of Michigan (opposed): Former President Gerald Ford, former Senator Bob Dole, and other Republicans have called on Congressional leaders to permit a censure vote. . . . It is tragically unfair that the opportunity for at least half of our members to vote our conscience will not be allowed. (H 11973)

Curiously, in this battle for the voices of Ford and Dole, their endorsement of censure moved from initially being a claim to ultimately being more of a fact simply by being repeated as such by rhetors opposed to impeachment.

Former Representative Barbara Jordan entered the debate in Californian Anna Eshoo's statement. She reminded listeners how Jordan had invoked the Constitution as "the soul of our Nation" during the 1974 impeachment hearings. Representative James Rogan, also of California, a few minutes later tried to claim the voice of Jordan for the pro-impeachment side. He noted that Eshoo had "invoked the name of our venerated late former colleague, the gentlewoman from Texas, Democrat Barbara Jordan." Then, he reminded his audience of who Jordan was and how she had first come to national attention during the Judiciary Committee hearings on the impeachment of Richard Nixon. Then, he quoted her. The *Congressional Record*'s editors do not make it clear where her words ended and his resumed, perhaps because he ellided her voice with his:

Congresswoman Jordan said during the Nixon hearing, "It is wrong, I suggest, it is a misreading of the Constitution, for any member here to assert that for a member to vote for an article of impeachment means that the member must be convinced that the President should be removed from office. The Constitution does not say that. The powers relating to impeachment are an essential check in the hands of this body, the legislature, against and upon the encroachment of the executive. In establishing the division between the two branches of the legislature, the House and the Senate, assigning to one the right to accuse and to the other the right to judge, the framers of the Constitution were very astute. They did not make the accusers and the judges the same person." (H 11845)

Representative Brian Bilbray of California repeated Rogan's point later in the debate: "[A]s Ms. Jordan pointed out in 1974, it is a misreading of the Constitution for any Member here to assert that a Member is voting to remove the President" (H 11941). So did others who favored impeachment. Very late in the debate, Representative Sheila Jackson-Lee, who served the same Texas district as Jordan had, attemped to reclaim the eloquent late Congresswoman's voice. Jackson-Lee said, "I have been careful not to mischaracterize her thoughts or words during these serious and troubling times. However, throughout the debate it seems at every moment the Republican majority continues to misuse Ms. Jordan's comments." Jackson-Lee then quoted Jordan's views on when impeachment was appropriate: when "a President [is] swollen with power and grown tyrannical" or when a President "attempts to subvert the Constitution" (H 12040). These conditions do not, Jackson-Lee argued, exist in 1998.

Surprisingly, the voice of Lincoln was also fought over. At the debate's beginning, Illinois' Henry Hyde quoted Lincoln's 1838 address to the Young Men's Lyceum. In this address, Hyde tells us, Lincoln "celebrated the rule of law" (H 11777). Missouri's Gephart, speaking just moments later, had the Lincoln who paid tribute to "government of the people, by the people" at Gettysburg in mind. Gephart asked that the people's voices be heard. Representative William Jefferson of Louisiana had still another Lincoln in mind, the Lincoln who tried to hold a dissolving nation together. Partisan bickering and the perversion of the constitutional provision for impeachment by Republican zealots were, in 1998, endangering the nation. Lincoln's voice cried out through Jefferson's citation for an end to such dangerous political action. Representative Steven Chabot of Ohio had still another Lincoln in mind, the Lincoln who said, "let us dare to do our duty as we understand it" (H 11836). According to Chabot, that duty, in 1998, was to impeach Bill Clinton.

Ohio's Kucinich seemed to agree with Representative Jefferson's use of Lincoln's voice. Representative Jay Dickey of Arkansas had a Lincoln yet unheard from in mind—the Abe who will chop down the stately tree should he find it hollow to save those who might be killed should it fall. The nation with Clinton as its leader was that hollow tree, according to Dickey. Massachusetts' William Delahunt had yet one more Lincoln to voice, the Lincoln who supported censure of President Polk. Lincoln's endorsement proved that the House may censure a president, contrary to the claim of pro-impeachment Republicans.

The line between quoting and stylizing an authority is sometimes difficult to draw. Some of the attempts above to sound Lincoln's voice on behalf of one position or another might better be characterized as stylizations. Other stylizations appeared in the debate. For example, Representative Eshoo of California stylized Franklin Roosevelt's call for a declaration of war against Japan. In her rendition, the Republicans had replaced the Japanese pilots who launched the sneak attack on Pearl Harbor (H 11842). And Massachusetts Representative Joseph Kennedy stylized Lyndon Johnson.

LBJ's words, "Let us continue," uttered after Kennedy's uncle's assassination, rang through in young Kennedy's call for the nation to get about its important business (H 11801).

There was also a great deal of prosopopoeia used by the different sides in the impeachment debate. Democrats parodically produced imagined words that Republicans are saying; both those opposed to and those in favor of impeachment produced the imagined words constituents were speaking. Perhaps most interesting were the imagined words the House will be uttering, according to pro-impeachment speakers, by its vote:

KENNY HULSHOF of Missouri (in favor): America surrendered the rule of law. (H 11799)

BILL McCOLLUM of Florida (in favor): [W]e have a double standard in this country, that the President, who is the chief law enforcement officer, the Commander in Chief of the uniformed services of this country, is allowed to get away with perjury. (H 11805)

JAMES HANSEN of Utah (in favor): Our peaceful and deliberate defense of the Constitution and its foundation in the rule of law will send a strong and clear message, testifying to the power and resilience of our democracy. Tyrants, dictators, and thugs around the world will see the strength of our Nation lies not in one man but in a vast people, united in liberty and justice. (H 11826)

RICK LAZIO of New York (in favor): With our votes we will send a compelling message one way or the other to the children in classrooms across this country who are watching their democracy at work. We are going to teach them through our words and through our deeds either to respect or to have contempt for the truth. This will be the timeless legacy of this Congress. (H 11837)

RON PACKARD of California (in favor): We must send a message, that no one, no matter how powerful or how popular, is above the law. (H 11865)

These proponents of impeachment, although they perhaps "lost" the voices of Ford and Dole, won when it came to announcing the imagined message the House was about to send.

As Lazio's prosopopoeia suggested, many speakers expressed concern about the children who were watching or would ask about the impeachment deliberations. Some of the most effective stories Representatives told during the debate were brief ones about these children. Given the time limitations the Representatives were under, many of these stories were really not much more than the barest hints of a tale. For example, when Bob Schaffer of California said, "I want my children to know that when their father lectures them to tell the truth, he means it" (H 11916), or when Connie Morella of Maryland said, "As a mother and grandmother, I struggled mightily with what message we send to all our children if the President does not bare serious consequence for his dishonest behavior" (H 11936), we entered just a bit into the stories of these legislators' personal lives.

Fuller still are the abbreviated stories told by North Carolina's Sue Myrick, Wisconsin's Ron Kind, Ohio's Steven Chabot, and New York's Michael Forbes:

MYRICK: Mr. Speaker, just before the November 3 election, my 5–year-old grandson, Jake, asked his mother if we were going to be electing a new President, and upon being told, no, we already have a President, Jake replied: No, we do not; he lied. (H 11809)

KIND: Mr. Speaker, I have two young boys who are not old enough yet to comprehend the gravity of this situation. My only hope is when they are old enough and are reading about this in the history books, that they are going to have confidence that every vote cast was done in the best interests of the country, rather than short-term political gain. (H 11834)

CHABOT: I have two children at home, a daughter and a son. With the help of their teachers and their church, my wife and I have tried to teach them about honesty and integrity. We have tried to instill in them a belief that character does indeed matter. We have taught them to obey the law. Sadly, they have seen these principles corrupted by the chief law enforcement officer of this land, the President of the United States. William Jefferson Clinton has disgraced his sacred office, he has cheapened the oath, he has disillusioned an entire generation of young Americans, and he refuses to accept responsibility for his actions. (H 11836)

FORBES: I include for the *Record* a letter that I wrote to my children this morning:

Dear Abby, Ted and Sam: Tomorrow, I will cast a difficult vote to impeach the President of the United States. . . . I always taught you to tell the truth. You have never disappointed me and I am proud to be your dad. Years from now, when you look back on the vote your father cast, I know you will understand the importance of my decision. And, I hope you will understand that I did it for you—for the country you will inherit, live in and lead. (H 11905)

These stories then were not as extensive as, for example, the ones we found Barbara Boxer and Paul Simon telling about women whose lives were saved by late-term abortions. These stories were also much more personal: the legislators are offering their stories as fathers, mothers, and grandmothers as representative of the millions of stories out there in America. And, although Morella and Kind opposed impeachment, these stories, as a group, seemed to be bringing the stories and voices of these children much more into the debate on behalf of those who were advocating the most stringent punishment of Bill Clinton.

DOUBLE-VOICING AND CARNIVALESQUE

Schaffer, Myrick, Chabot, and Forbes all sounded very sincere as they delivered these words about their families. In fact, much of the speaking against the president was characterized by a comparably sincere tone. However, some who opposed the president were certainly veiling a much more partisan political agenda beneath their talk about values and law. The pro-impeachment voices were disciplined enough not to reveal their double-voiced discourse. We know, however, that the partisan agenda is operative because of the highly-politicized context in which the impeachment drama had been played out and because anti-impeachment speakers were not at all reluctant to expose the partisan political agenda of their opponents during the debate on December 18 and 19.

Here are some samples of what anti-impeachment speakers said:

EDWARD MARKEY of Massachusetts: GOP used to stand for "Grand Old Party." Now, it just stands for "Get Our President." (H 11822)

WYNN: There is no bipartisanship on the floor, simply the will of this majority to drive out this president. . . . They talk about law, but they do not talk about justice. (H 11828–29)

BOBBY RUSH of Illinois: Mr. Speaker, the partisan politics being carried out by the Republican majority is a travesty being inflicted upon the American people. . . . The Gestapo-like tactics employed by the Republican majority are reminiscent of some of the darkest chapters in history, as with the Spanish Inquisition and Nazi Germany. (H 11908)

EDDIE JOHNSON of Texas: We have spent $40 million of the taxpayer's money for the Republicans to be able to say "gotcha." (H 11914)

GARY ACKERMAN of New York: Mr. Speaker, today we embarrass the memory of our Founding Fathers as we torture the intent of the genius of their system of balancing the awesome powers of government. Mr. Speaker, under your leadership and that of your party we stand here, small men with petty careers and partisan of purpose to diminish yet again our great Republic. Devoid of a sense of proportion and overburdened with an excess of hubris, you claim conscience as your exclusive domain and deny us the right to offer the will of the people, a motion to censure. Your oligarchical act attempts to recreate a presidency that would serve at your whim rather than at the will of the people. (H 11938)

SERRANO: From day one they [the Republican right wing] wanted to get rid of Bill Clinton. From day one they stood on him and tried to make him out to be the number one villain in this country. They have been blinded by hate then and they are blinded by hate today. This place is full of hate because of what they tried to do to our president. (H 11970)

Representative Loretta Sanchez of California gave the argument a personal twist because she had been "the target of a blatantly partisan investigation," one intended to deprive her of her seat in Congress. "They tried to undo that election," she said, "and now they are trying to undo the President's election" (H 11911). And Representative Jesse Jackson, Jr., of Illinois gave the argument a racial twist, accusing the Republican majority of using language "laced with not-so-subtle new racial code words" (H 11810) to attack Clinton who stood for social programs vital to the continued economic development of African Americans:

Let us not be confused. Today Republicans are impeaching Social Security, they are impeaching affirmative action, they are impeaching women's right to choose. Medicare, Medicaid, Supreme Court Justices who believe in equal protection under the law for all Americans. Something deeper in history is happening than sex, lying about sex and perjury. In 1868 it was about reconstruction, and in 1998 it is still about reconstruction. . . . Today's conservative southern-based Republicans' target is the Second Reconstruction, especially the "liberalism" of Democratic President Lyndon Johnson's Great Society but also ultimately including many of the "Big Government" programs of Franklin Delano Roosevelt's New Deal. The real underlying dynamic of this impeachment proceeding is not the removal of Bill Clinton, but the removal of the social and economic programs of the New Deal and the Second Reconstruction of the Great Society, a weakening of the Big Federal Government generally, and the destruction of liberalism as a viable political ideology in particular. (H 11809–10)

A certain amount of carnivalesque energy developed as some anti-impeachment speakers offered such rhetoric. However, there was sufficient division among those speakers that they did not coalesce as a minority group intent upon subverting the will of the Republican majority in the House. One fundamental division, for example, separated those who condemned Clinton but asked for censure and those who defended Clinton as a victim of right-wing Republican zealots.

Within the confines of the House, the anti-impeachment forces were indeed the minority. However, in the larger national context, the House Republican majority was the disempowered group. They had lost the White House in 1992 and in 1996; they had been badly bruised by Clinton when they shut down the government rather than compromise on their legislative agenda. As a disempowered group, carnivalesque energy is available to them. And bringing down the president—especially when accompanied by revelations that stripped the president of the dignity of his office—was certainly a carnivalesque occasion. However, the insistence of the leaders of the pro-impeachment forces on dignity—so as not to foreground partisan politics—inhibited displays of such energy. It is difficult to insist with seriousness on the rule of law and, simultaneously, engage in carnivalesque behavior, which favors misrule over rule. Then, Livingston's announcement on Saturday morning, as noted earlier, seemed to put a damper on any carnivalesque energy that might have been ready to spark a fire.

LACK OF FINALIZABILITY

The debate on that Friday and Saturday in December 1998 was neatly packaged by the House leadership with C-SPAN and other media in mind. As neat as that package might have seemed, the debate extended beyond the established temporal bounds in both directions. It extended back to the impeachment of Andrew Johnson, the near-impeachment of Richard Nixon, and to House actions against Jim Wright and Newt Gingrich. All of these prior events were brought into the 1998 debate, as were the elections of 1992 and 1996.

The debate also, in the view of many speakers, extended into the future. Many on the anti-impeachment side spoke specifically about how this debate would affect the future. Diana Degette of Colorado, early in the debate, declared that

> This vote is unworthy of our institution. We will pay for it in the years
> to come. We will undermine the ability of the next generation of
> American presidents to lead us through the enormous challenges that

face the 21st Century, just as we did after the last impeachment of a President over 100 years ago. (H 11795)

Her fears for the future were stated in vague terms. Edward Markey of Massachusetts was more specific in his forecast:

> We are permitting a constitutional coup d'etat which will haunt this body forever. A constitutional clause intended to apply to a Benedict Arnold selling out his country will now be expanded to cover every personal transgression. Every future President, Democrat or Republican, will be subject to harrassment by his political enemies, who can credibly threaten impeachment for the slightest misconduct. (H 11822)

Ruben Hinojosa of Texas concurred. The House's action would "lower the threshold for impeachment for all future Presidents" and thereby "pose a threat to the system of checks and balances and separation of powers that form the foundation of our system of democratic governance" (H 11863).

Several speakers praised how former New Jersey Congressman Peter Rodino had conducted the hearings that led to articles of impeachment against President Richard Nixon. Care was taken at every turn to make sure the process was not unduly politicized. As Representative Donald Payne of New Jersey noted, "During the Watergate hearings in 1974, Chairman Rodino won the respect and admiration of the entire Nation for his insistence on fairness, his profound respect for the U.S. Constitution and his impeccable sense of decorum" (H 11861). That care, several noted, was not apparent in 1998—either in committee or on the House floor. That lack of care will, these speakers say, lead to more debates over impeachment and more fractious debates over impeachment. Matters certainly were not finalized with the vote on December 19th. Neither were they finalized after the subsequent Senate trial. If those speaking against the impeachment of William Jefferson Clinton were in any degree correct, the debate on December 18th and 19th continued and intensified a constitutional and political debate over the impeachment process itself.

Works Cited

Bakhtin, Mikhail. *The Dialogic Imagination: Four Essays.* Ed. Michael Holquist. Austin: University of Texas Press, 1981.

———. *Problems of Dostoevsky's Poetics.* Trans. and ed. Caryl Emerson. Minneapolis: University of Minnesota Press, 1984.

———. *Rabelais and His World.* Trans. Helene Iswolsky. Bloomington: Indiana University Press, 1984.

Bauer, Dale M. *Feminist Dialogics: A Theory of Failed Community.* Albany: SUNY Press, 1998.

Bauer, Dale M., and Susan Jaret McKinstry. *Feminism, Bakhtin, and the Dialogic.* Albany: SUNY Press, 1991.

Bernard-Donals, Michael. "Mikhail Bakhtin: Between Phenomenology and Marxism." In *Landmark Essays on Bakhtin, Rhetoric, and Writing.* Ed. Frank Farmer. Mahwah, NJ: Hermagoras, 1998. 63–79.

———. "Mikhail Bakhtin, Classical Rhetoric, and Praxis." In *Landmark Essays on Bakhtin, Rhetoric, and Writing.* Ed. Frank Farmer. Mahwah, NJ: Hermagoras, 1998. 105–11.

Bialostosky, Don. "Bakhtin and the Future of Rhetorical Criticism." In *Landmark Essays on Bakhtin, Rhetoric, and Writing.* Ed. Frank Farmer. Mahwah, NJ: Hermagoras, 1998. 111–17.

Bormann, Ernest. "The Southern Senators' Filibuster on Civil Rights: Speechmaking as Parliamentary Strategy." *Southern Speech Journal* 27 (1962): 183–94.

Bowman, Michael S. "'Novelizing' the Stage: Chamber Theatre after Brea and Bakhtin." *Text and Performance Quarterly* 15 (1995): 1–23.

Braden, Waldo W. "The Senate Debate on the League of Nations, 1918–1920: An Overview." *Southern Speech Journal* 25 (1960): 273–81.

Butler, John. "Carol Moseley-Braun's Day to Talk about Race: A Study of Forum in the United States Senate." *Argumentation and Advocacy* 32 (1995): 62–74.

Cahn, D. Dudley, Edward J. Pappas, and Ladene Schoen. "Speech in the Senate: 1978." *Communication Quarterly* 27 (Summer 1979): 50–54.

Cain, Earl R. "A Method for Rhetorical Analysis of Congressional Debate." *Western Speech* 18 (March 1954): 91–95.

———. "Is Senate Debate Significant?" *Today's Speech* 3 (April 1955): 10–12, 26–27.

———. "Obstacles to Early Congressional Reporting." *Southern Speech Journal* 27 (1962): 239–47.

Campbell, Karlyn Kohrs, and Kathleen Hall Jamieson. *Deeds Done in Words: Presidential Rhetoric and the Genres of Governance*. Chicago: University of Chicago Press, 1990.

Carlson, Margaret. "Seeing Stars over Kelso." *Time*, May 2, 1994: 68.

Carlson, Marvin. "Theater and Dialogism." In *Critical Theory and Performance*. Ed. Janelle G. Reinelt and Joseph R. Roach. Ann Arbor: University of Michigan Press, 1992. 313–23.

Chester, Giraud. "Contemporary Senate Debate: A Case Study." *Quarterly Journal of Speech* 31 (1945): 407–11.

Conquergood, Dwight. "Performance and Dialogical Understanding: In Quest of the Other." In *Communication as Performance*. Ed. Janet L. Palmer. Tempe: Arizona State University, 1986. 30–37.

———. "Performance as a Moral Act: Ethical Dimensions of the Ethnography of Performance." *Literature in Performance* 5.2 (1985): 1–13.

Cooper, Marilyn M. "Dialogic Learning across Disciplines." In *Landmark Essays on Bakhtin, Rhetoric, and Writing*. Ed. Frank Farmer. Mahwah, NJ: Hermagoras, 1998. 81–95.

Davis, Richard. *The Press and American Politics: The New Mediator*. New York: Longman, 1992.

———. "Whither the Congress and the Supreme Court? The Television News Portrayal of American National Government." *Television Quarterly* 22 (1987): 55–63.

Dewar, Helen. "Helms vs. Moseley-Braun, Again." *Washington Post,* October 19, 1999: A17.

———. "Late-Term Abortion Ban Passes." *Washington Post,* October 22, 1999: A4.

Farmer, Frank. "Introduction." In *Landmark Essays on Bakhtin, Rhetoric, and Writing*. Ed. Frank Farmer. Mahwah, NJ: Hermagoras, 1998. xi–xxiii.

Fisher, Walter R. "The Failure of Compromise in 1860–61: A Rhetorical View." *Speech Monographs* 33 (1966): 364–71.

Fitzpatrick, John R. "Congressional Debating." *Quarterly Journal of Speech* 27 (1941): 251–55.

Halasek, Kay. "Feminism and Bakhtin: Dialogic Reading in the Academy." In *Landmark Essays on Bahktin, Rhetoric, and Writing*. Ed. Frank Farmer. Mahwah, NJ: Hermagoras, 1998. 51–62.

———. "Starting the Dialogue: What Can We Do About Bakhtin's Ambivalence Toward Rhetoric?" *In Landmark Essays on Bakhtin, Rhetoric, and Writing*. Ed. Frank Farmer. Mahwah, NJ: Hermagoras, 1998. 97–105.

Harmon, William, and C. Hugh Holman. *A Handbook to Literature*. 7th ed. Upper Saddle River, NJ: Prentice Hall, 1996.

Harris, R. Allen. "Bakhtin, *Phaedrus*, and the Geometry of Rhetoric." In *Landmark Essays on Bakhtin, Rhetoric, and Writing*. Ed. Frank Farmer. Mahwah, NJ: Hermagoras, 1998. 15–22.

Hart, Roderick P. *Verbal Style and the Presidency: A Computer-Based Analysis*. Orlando, FL: Academic Press, 1984.

Hendrix, J. A. "A New Look at Textual Authenticity of Speeches in Congressional Record." *Southern Speech Journal* 31 (1965): 153.

Holquist, Michael. *Dialogism: Bakhtin and His World*. London: Routledge, 1990.

HopKins, Mary Frances. "From Page to Stage: The Burden of Proof." *Southern Speech Communication Journal* 47 (1981): 1–9.

HopKins, Mary Frances, and Brent Bouldin. "Professional Group Performance of Non-Dramatic Literature in New York." In *Performance of Literature in Historical Perspectives*. Ed. David W. Thompson. Lanham, MD: University Press of America, 1983. 697–717.

Hoy, Mikita. "Joyful Mayhem: Bakhtin, Football Songs, and the Carnivalesque." *Text and Performance Quarterly* 14 (1994): 289–304.

Hutcheon, Linda. *A Theory of Parody: The Teaching of Twentieth Century Art Forms*. New York: Routledge, 1985.

Jamieson, Kathleen Hall. Carroll C. Arnold Lecture. National Communication Association, Chicago. November 4, 1999.

Jansinski, James. "The Forms and Limits of Prudence in Henry Clay's 1850 Defense of the Compromise Measures." *Quarterly Journal of Speech* 81 (1995): 454–78.

Johnson, F. "Friendships among Women: Closeness in Dialogue." In *Gendered Relationships*. Ed. Julia T. Wood. Mountain View, CA: Mayfield, 1996. 79–94.

Kane, Peter. "Extended Debate and the Rules of the United States Senate." *Quarterly Journal of Speech* 57 (1971): 43–49.

Kane, Thomas. "Argumentation and the U.S. Senate." *Argumentation and Advocacy* 32 (1995): 57–61.

Kent, Thomas. "Hermeneutics and Genre: Bakhtin and the Problem of Communicative Interaction." In *Landmark Essays on Bakhtin, Rhetoric, and Writing*. Ed. Frank Farmer. Mahwah, NJ: Hermagoras, 1998. 33–49.

Klancher, Jon. "Bakhtin's Rhetoric." In *Landmark Essays on Bakhtin, Rhetoric, and Writing*. Ed. Frank Farmer. Mahwah, NJ: Hermagoras, 1998. 23–32.

Kraus, Sidney. *Televised Presidential Debates and Public Policy*. 2nd ed. Mahwah, NJ: Lawrence Erlbaum Associates, 2000.

Kristeva, Julia. "Word, Dialogue and Novel." In *The Kristeva Reader*. Ed. Toril Moi. New York: Columbia University Press, 1986. 34–61.

Lewis, E. T., and P. R. McCarthy, "Perceptions of Self-Disclosure as a Function of Gender-Linked Variables." *Sex Roles* 19 (1988): 47–56.

McPherson, Elizabeth G. "Reporting the Debating of Congress." *Quarterly Journal of Speech* 28 (1942): 141–48.

Micken, Ralph A. "The Triumph of Strategy in the Senate Debate on the League of Nations." *Quarterly Journal of Speech* 37 (1951): 49–53.

———. "Western Senators in the League of Nations Debate, 1919–1920." *Western Speech* 16 (October 1952): 239–44.

Miller, Arthur H., Edie N. Goldenberg, and Lutz Erbring. "Type-Set Politics: The Impact of Newspapers on Public Confidence." *American Political Science Review* 73 (1979): 67–84.

Montgomery, Kirt E. "Thomas B. Reed's Theory and Practice of Congressional Debating." *Speech Monographs* 17 (March 1950): 65–74.

Morson, Gary Saul, and Caryl Emerson. *Mikhail Bakhtin: Creation of a Prosaics*. Stanford, CA: Stanford University Press, 1990.

Murphy, John M. "Critical Rhetoric as Political Discourse." *Argumentation and Advocacy* 32 (1995): 1–15.

"Navy to Restore Ties to Tailhook." *Washington Post*, January 20, 2000: A7.

Palmer, Linda. "Senate Backs Admiral's Pension over Women's Opposition." *Congressional Quarterly*, April 23, 1994: 1014.

Park-Fuller, Linda M. "Voices: Bakhtin's Heteroglossia and Polyphony, and the Performance of Narrative Literature." *Literature in Performance* 7.1 (1986): 1–12.

Popovich, Vasile. "Is the Stage-Audience Relationship a Form of Dialogue?" *Poetics* 13 (1984): 111–18.

Pressley, Sue Anne. "Boycott Aims to Bring Flag Down." *Washington Post*, August 2, 1999: A3.

Quadro, David F. "Another Look." *Western Journal of Communication* 41 (1977): 253–59.

Raspberry, William. "Symbolic Arguments." *Washington Post*, August 2, 1999: A19.

Richter, David. "Bakhtin in Life and in Art." *Style* (Fall 1986): 411–19.

Robinson, Michael J., and Kevin R. Appel. "Network News Coverage of Congress." *Political Science Quarterly* 94 (1979): 407–18.

Robinson, Zon. "Are Speeches in Congressional Reports Accurate?" *Quarterly Journal of Speech* 28 (1942): 8–12.

Saurer, M. K., and R. M. Eisler. "The Role of Masculine Gender Roles Stress in Expressivity and Social Support Network Factors." *Sex Roles* 23 (1990): 261–71.

Scheele, Henry Z. "Some Reactions by Congressmen to Speaking in the U.S. House of Representatives." *Today's Speech* 14 (February 1966): 19–21.

Schuetz, Janice. "Overlays of Argument in Legislative Process." *Journal of the American Forensic Association* 22 (1986): 223–34.

Schuster, Charles I. "Mikhail Bakhtin as Rhetorical Theorist." In *Landmark Essays on Bakhtin, Rhetoric, and Writing*. Ed. Frank Farmer. Mahwah, NJ: Hermagoras, 1998. 1–14.

Sheckels, Theodore F. "The Rhetorical Use of Double-Voiced Discourse and Feminine Style: The U.S. Senate Debate over the Impact of Tailhook '91 on Admiral Frank B. Kelso II's Retirement Rank." *Southern Communication Journal* 63 (1997): 56–68.

Smith, Craig Allen. *Political Communication*. San Diego: Harcourt Brace Jovanovich, 1990.

Stevens, Wallace W. "Inaccuracies in the Texts of Congressional Speeches." *Communication Studies* 15 (1964): 183–88.

Tannen, Deborah. *You Just Don't Understand: Women and Men in Conversation*. New York: William Morrow, 1990.

Tidmarch, Charles, and John C. Pitney, Jr. "Covering Congress." *Polity* 17 (1985): 463–83.

Vatz, Richard E., and Theodore Otto Windt, Jr. "The Defeats of Judges Haynsworth and Carswell: Rejection of Supreme Court Nominees." *Quarterly Journal of Speech* 60 (1974): 477–88.

Voorhis, Jerry. "Effective Speaking in Congress." *Quarterly Journal of Speech* 34 (1948): 462–63.

Wood, J. T., and C. Inman. "In a Different Mode: Recognizing Male Modes of Closeness." *Journal of Applied Communication Research* 21 (1993): 279–95.

Zebroski, James Thomas. "Mikhail Bakhtin and the Question of Rhetoric." In *Landmark Essays on Bakhtin, Rhetoric, and Writing*. Ed. Frank Farmer. Mahwah, NJ: Hermagoras, 1998. 117–125.

Zulick, Margaret D. "The Agon of Jeremiah: On the Dialogical Invention of Prophetic Ethos." *Quarterly Journal of Speech* 78 (1992): 125–48.

———. "Pursuing Controversy: Kristeva's Split Subject, Bakhtin's Many-Tongued World." *Argumentation and Advocacy* 28 (1991): 91–102.

Index

About the Author

THEODORE F. SHECKELS is Professor of English and Communication at Randolph-Macon College. He is the author of *Debating: Applied Rhetorical Theory* (1984) and *The Lion on the Freeway: A Thematic Introduction to Contemporary South African Literature in English* (1996).